No Biting

THIRD EDITION

Other Redleaf Press books by Gretchen Kinnell

Good Going! Successful Potty Training for Children in Child Care

Good Going! The Potty Training Guide for Families

Why Children Bite: A Family Companion to "No Biting"

NO BITING

THIRD EDITION

Solutions and Support for Toddler Programs

Gretchen Kinnell

for Child Care Solutions

 **Redleaf Press®**
www.redleafpress.org
800-423-8309

Published by Redleaf Press
10 Yorkton Court
St. Paul, MN 55117
www.redleafpress.org

Senior editor: Heidi Hogg

Managing editor: Douglas Schmitz

First edition published 2002. Third edition 2019.

Cover design: Charles Rue Woods and Jim Handrigan

Cover photograph: iStock.com/mbot

Interior design: Louise OFarrell

Typeset in Adobe Minion Pro

Printed in the United States of America

26 25 24 23 22 21 20 19   1 2 3 4 5 6 7 8

Library of Congress Cataloging-in-Publication Data

Names: Kinnell, Gretchen, 1950– author. | Child Care Solutions

Title: No biting : solutions and support for toddler programs / Gretchen Kinnell, for Child Care Solutions.

Description: Third edition. | St. Paul, MN : Redleaf Press, [2019]

Identifiers: LCCN 2018051794 (print) | LCCN 2018054326 (ebook) | ISBN 9781605546773 (e-book) | ISBN 9781605546766 (pbk. : alk. paper)

Subjects: LCSH: Toddlers—Development. | Toddlers—Psychology. | Children and violence.

Classification: LCC HQ774.5 (ebook) | LCC HQ774.5 .K56 2019 (print) | DDC 649/.122—dc23

LC record available at https://urldefense.proofpoint.com

Printed on acid-free paper

*To the teachers, caregivers, and administrators
who care for and about toddlers every day*

Contents

....

APPENDIX A

Sample Letters for Parents
and Policy Statements for Staff and Parents 107

APPENDIX B

Sample Observations 113

APPENDIX C

Incident Report Forms. 121

APPENDIX D

Curriculum for Staff Orientation and Training on Biting 131

APPENDIX E

Role-Playing to Help Staff Build Skills 181

Preface

The first edition of *No Biting* was the result of a task force formed to address biting. At the time, our organization was the Child Care Council of Onondaga County; in 2004 we changed our name to Child Care Solutions. For many years, we had provided technical assistance to programs and advice to parents on an individual basis. We found that many programs approached biting by trial and error, trying a string of techniques in rapid succession in the hopes they might stumble across something that would work. The caregivers involved often confided that they were not at all prepared to deal effectively with biting. They didn't understand why the toddlers were biting or why the techniques, which often included punishments, didn't work. They felt even more unsure of what to do when biting continued and they faced what they referred to as "biting epidemics."

Many programs and providers we worked with felt pressured to expel children who were biting. Directors felt caught between the parents and the staff and sometimes between the parents of the child who was biting and the parents of the children being bitten. Parents called us with complaints of incompetent caregivers and unresponsive directors. Other parents called in anguish because their children were being "kicked out of child care," some before they had turned two. And the toddlers themselves were caught in the middle of struggling programs and angry parents.

As we wrestled with these calls, we wished there were written materials we could send to parents, programs, and providers. We found that while we could find many articles, they were usually short, too general, or limited to just one aspect of biting, and all of them could only offer a few suggestions for how to cope with it. Much of the advice that was available was questionable and ineffective, and some was downright cruel. What we were looking for was a comprehensive resource for programs that carefully considered all the issues related to biting in toddler care settings and contained appropriate, effective suggestions for everyone involved: caregivers, administrators, and parents. Since we couldn't find one, we decided to convene a group of experienced toddler caregivers and program administrators to do the thinking, consider the issues, and create the resource we had been looking for.

This group became the Task Force on Biting and consisted of eighteen caregivers and administrators from child care centers and Early Head Start programs in Syracuse and surrounding Onondaga County. Over the course of several months in 1998, the members of the task force met regularly and created a process to develop the resource. They began by identifying what they wanted it to address. At first they thought they could simply gather the current information on biting, add some of their own thoughts and experiences, and organize it into a set of useful explanations of why toddlers bite and suggestions for how to stop it. What they found, however, was that they needed to go beyond simple explanations or solutions and grapple with the important issues at the heart of the biting dilemma: How do people look at biting? How do programs make decisions about their practices? How do programs deal with problem situations involving children? How do caregivers and programs respond to parents' concerns? How do programs respond to pressure from parents?

As the task force members worked through these issues, they realized that the discussions of the problems were as important as the resulting solutions. The Child Care Council decided to incorporate these discussions into a book so readers would understand the basis for the explanations, suggestions, strategies, and techniques.

Since the completion of the original task force's resource and the publication of the first edition of *No Biting*, Child Care Solutions has continued to work with programs, parents, and providers to address the dilemma of biting in child care programs serving toddlers. The second edition contained additional insights, information, suggestions, and sample observations that arose from helping child care programs tackle this important issue.

This third edition is based on the work of a focus group of directors and my consulting experiences with many early childhood programs that serve toddlers and their families. It incorporates their many suggestions and includes ready-to-use staff training resources, a new observation and reflection form, and a new chapter for infant-toddler specialists on consulting for biting. Finally, in response to many requests, resources from the appendixes are available at the *No Biting* product page at www.redleafpress.org.

Members of the Task Force on Biting, Child Care Solutions

Jennifer Burns	*Cazenovia Children's House*
Jackie Gower	*Cazenovia Children's House*
Gretchen Kinnell	*Child Care Council of Onondaga County*
Sherry Knepp	*Kids Unlimited Child Care Center*
Linda Leone	*Cazenovia Children's House*
Lynne Mathews	*Childtime Children's Center 0042*
Bev Meloon	*SonShine Child Care Center*
Nancy Meunier	*The Growing Place*
Pat Nye	*Marcellus Presbyterian Child Care Center*
Bonnie Phelps	*Child Care Council of Onondaga County*
Linda Ricks	*Early Head Start*
Tania Scholder	*Salvation Army—Clinton St. Day Care*
Bethany Scott	*SonShine Child Care Center*
Carol Taylor	*Early Head Start*
Alyce Thompson	*Salvation Army Day Care Services*
Sherry Abdul Wali	*Childtime Children's Center 0042*
Deb Warren	*O'Brien & Gere Child Care Center*
Jean Wells	*Marcellus Presbyterian Child Care Center*

Members of the focus group for the third edition of *No Biting*

Kristi Cusa	*Director of Professional Development, Child Care Solutions*
Sharon Morgan	*Director, Marcellus Community Child Care Center*
Tricia Narolis	*Early Learning Center Manager, Oneida Indian Nation*
Kelly Wentworth	*Executive Director, County North Children's Center, Inc.*

Acknowledgments

· ·

I would first like to acknowledge the commitment of the child care centers and especially the directors who sent their teachers and administrators to participate in the task force. It was their work that led to the first edition of *No Biting*.

I would like to acknowledge and thank the members of the focus group who helped shape this third edition. They were generous in sharing their expertise, experiences, insights, and suggestions for this edition.

Rothschild Early Childhood Center was especially generous in sharing their experiences for this third edition. Their willingness to dedicate time, thought, and resources to address biting is a model for other programs.

I would like to thank AIDS Community Resources in Syracuse, New York, for supplying research data and information on HIV/AIDS.

I would like to thank Dr. Gary Johnson, chair of emergency medicine at University Hospital in Syracuse, for information on appropriate first aid for biting.

I would like to recognize Redleaf Press for all its work to bring this and other resources to the early care and education community. I especially appreciate the work of David Heath, editor in chief, for his support ever since this book was first published. I would like to thank Lindsey Smith, my editor, who brought this third edition together and made so many of its materials accessible as web resources.

Finally, I thank the staff of Child Care Solutions for all the work they do to help child care programs and providers in our community work effectively with children and families and for their support of this book. I would especially like to recognize Kristi Cusa, director of professional development at Child Care Solutions, for developing the Biting Incident Documentation and Reflection Form and the accompanying guide. Her help with the focus group, her willingness to meet and grapple with ideas, and her careful review of the content are greatly appreciated.

Introduction

....

People who do not work with toddlers in groups might ask, "How can there be enough to say about biting to fill a book?" "Why would anyone need an entire book devoted to biting in toddler programs?" People who do work with toddlers in groups, and in all kinds of early childhood programs, however, never ask these questions. They know without a doubt that biting is a serious, complicated issue. They know because they struggle with it on a regular basis.

This was the opening paragraph of the first edition of *No Biting*. In the years since it was published in 2002, I have presented many workshops and some keynote addresses on biting. I have found that more and more people outside our field know that child care centers struggle with biting. They may not know exactly what the issues are, but they recognize biting as a problem. At a conference on biting held in New York, a local politician, Westchester County executive Andrew J. Spano, was being honored for his support of infant and toddler care. After looking over the conference agenda, which included my keynote, he told me that he hadn't known biting was such a serious issue. He had an interesting question: "What do I need to know about biting as the county executive? It must be pretty important if there is a whole conference about it." He wasn't a parent of a toddler, nor did he work in a child care program as a caregiver or an administrator, but as the county executive, he knew he should be concerned.

The answer to his question was that toddler biting is quite common in child care programs, yet even experienced caregivers often find it difficult to deal with. Both parents and caregivers can become frustrated and angry, sometimes to the point that when they can't come up with a solution, a toddler may be expelled from child care. Parents who are embroiled in difficult biting situations at a center or child care home are likely to miss work—especially those who must find new child care. That means there are not only unhappy parents but also unhappy employers.

Helping caregivers and administrators address biting more effectively with toddlers and their parents is important not just to child care programs and the families they serve but to the whole community.

At Child Care Solutions, we have long been aware that biting is an ongoing and difficult issue in child care programs. We know this because we have more calls from programs, providers, and parents about biting than about any other issue. In our experience, no other single issue in programs for toddlers inflames parents and frustrates staff the way biting does. Of course parents don't want their children to be injured in any way by another toddler, but they are usually understanding and supportive of caregivers while they work to resolve problems like pinching, hitting, or even kicking. The reaction to biting, however, is usually different. Flesh torn by teeth seems so primal, so animalistic, and so frightening that it evokes very strong feelings in adults. There's still a little distance when children hit each other, but biting is up close and personal. We have seen adults completely lose control over biting—crying, cursing, even threatening staff or other parents. The most understanding and supportive parents can become exasperated when biting continues and nothing works to stop it.

It has been more than fifteen years since Redleaf Press first published *No Biting*. In that time, I have revised the book once, developed the family companion booklet, conducted countless workshops on biting, done many consultations with programs on biting, and retired from Child Care Solutions where I had worked for twenty-three years. When I was asked to consider a third edition of the book, it was not difficult to come up with a process for the revision. *No Biting* was originally the work of a task force in central New York, so it made sense to go back to the local early childhood community for insights, comments, and suggestions. Together with the new director of professional development at Child Care Solutions, we held a small focus group of local child care center directors. All were familiar with the book; all had used and continue to use it as a guide in their programs. They were willing to share their reflections on and experiences with biting situations. They also discussed how *No Biting* had shaped their work with children, parents, and staff.

We began by asking them, "What are you currently seeing and experiencing in your programs related to biting?" From the responses and discussion that followed, three things emerged that everyone agreed on. Two were aspects of biting that they felt had not changed at all since the 2002 publication of *No Biting*, and one was a very important aspect that they felt had changed a great deal.

Here is what they felt had not changed:

- ▶ Toddlers still bite.
- ▶ Parents are still surprised and upset when their children bite or are bitten.

Here is what they felt *had* changed:

- ▶ They and their staff feel confident that they can deal with biting successfully when it does happen. As one director said, "We know we're going to see biting, but it's not as dreaded. We know we can be effective."

These responses are significant for several reasons. The first statement supports the understanding that biting is not unexpected during the toddler developmental stage. This understanding is a foundation of *No Biting* and is expressed clearly in the perspective on biting that "when toddlers are in groups, biting is unfortunately not unexpected." The directors and caregivers accepted the likelihood that biting might happen in their toddler rooms. In doing so, they accepted that it was up to them to develop effective practices to address biting if and when it did occur.

The second statement confirms that biting remains emotionally charged for many parents. That hasn't changed, and it isn't likely to. Just as we can't reasonably expect that all toddler biting will stop, we cannot reasonably expect that parents will not be upset when it does happen. When directors and caregivers realized and accepted this, they could choose not to take parents' emotional reactions personally or respond defensively. They could respond to parents with understanding and then focus on communication, information, and interventions to address the biting. Directors reported that developing this understanding and sharing it with staff relieved some of the stress of biting situations and helped everyone move forward.

So biting hasn't changed and parents' responses haven't changed. And that is why the third statement is especially important. Directors and caregivers feel that they know what to do when biting occurs. They still wish it wouldn't happen, but they know how they can reduce the likelihood of biting, and they know how they can work with toddlers effectively so biting does not continue or escalate. The directors attributed this to *No Biting*. They found the perspective on biting to be a valuable starting point in their own thinking and in training their staff. The information on the reasons toddlers might bite put an end to staff convictions and declarations that a child had bitten "for no reason." They cited specific practices in the book that they felt had helped reduce biting in their centers; for example, more sensory activities and more different textures in their menus. They began to use observations to gain insights into specific biting situations. Staff members who were familiar with the information in *No Biting* were able to help new staff. And, finally, directors appreciated the information on policies for biting.

Their responses to *No Biting* mirror those of the many directors I have encountered since the book was first published. While this is gratifying, it is even more important that these directors have thought more about biting, identified issues, and made valuable suggestions to make *No Biting* even more useful. This third edition incorporates the insights and suggestions of the directors along with my own ideas and experiences working with toddler caregivers, directors, and parents. It builds on the work of the original task force, which continues to stand us in good stead.

Describing Biting

The members of the original task force found that the words they used to describe the problem of biting among toddlers shaped the way they thought about the issue. They needed to have a common understanding of biting and a common language to discuss the problem of biting in order to choose responses and develop policies. As a result, the task force struggled with how to describe or label biting. It certainly qualifies as a behavior problem, but it's different from many other common behavior problems. While many toddlers bite, the causes vary, so many traditional discipline techniques do not work. Since biting is often associated with the toddler stage and many toddlers bite, task force members considered referring to biting as *normal* or *typical*. They felt that both of these words implied something that all children would do, something providers should be looking for as an indication that a child's development was proceeding as it should. Logically, then, a child who didn't bite would be seen as a child who was not on target developmentally. Since that obviously isn't true, the task force decided not to use *normal* or *typical* to describe biting.

Task force members then tried thinking of biting from the providers' point of view and found that many of them considered it an expected behavior. Using the word *expected*, however, didn't seem to be a very good way to talk with parents about biting. Most parents do not expect toddlers to bite, and it seemed unlikely that parents would want their children in a program that expected biting to occur. Calling biting *expected* seemed to portray it as unavoidable, which might imply to parents that it would be taken too lightly. It might even conjure up images of caregivers eagerly awaiting the expected biting.

The task force finally settled on describing biting as a toddler behavior that is "unfortunately not unexpected." This conveys the understanding that while biting is not something providers or administrators want for the children in their programs and is not something they look forward to, the staff in good programs are not surprised by biting among toddlers and are prepared to address it.

However you refer to biting in your program, this experience taught us that it is necessary to talk about biting among staff members until you find words that make sense to everyone. In the process, you may uncover differences in your assumptions about biting that can make it difficult to reach consensus on a plan to address it.

Assumptions about Biting

Most people (certainly most parents) see biting as a behavior problem that must be punished. Some adults believe that biting is a crime that calls for justice. According to this way of thinking, if there is no punishment, then the biter has gotten away with it, and this cannot be allowed. Parents are often infuriated when they see their own child bruised by a bite mark and no evidence of anyone serving time for the crime. They may express shock and disbelief when they ask what happened to the child who bit and learn that the child was told, "We don't bite," and then redirected to another area of the room. Many parents, and a number of providers, may want the child who bit to have to pay a price for biting. Punishment makes them feel that in at least some small way, justice has been served. This places tremendous pressure on administrators and programs to punish biting to the satisfaction of adults, both providers and parents. Programs focused on the needs of children, however, do not use techniques simply to satisfy the adults involved when those techniques are, in fact, inappropriate or ineffective with children. And there's a lot of research showing that punishment is not an effective response to *any* kind of behavior problem.

While the task force took the position that biting is never justified, they also recognized that most of the many reasons toddlers bite do not fall into traditional "crime and punishment" or even "problem behavior and consequences" models of addressing challenging behaviors. While everyone's goal is to help toddlers stop biting and learn other behavior, punishing the child who is biting does not help anyone—the child, the provider, or the parent—reach that goal. It's that simple. What *is* effective at helping toddlers stop biting? To answer that question, it's necessary to understand why toddlers bite and then find strategies and techniques that match the child's reason or reasons for biting. Only then will the biting stop.

The real challenge for programs is to address biting effectively with children and explain it effectively to adults. In this book you will find information, strategies, techniques, and suggestions to do just that.

Is Biting Bullying?

Directors report that both parents and staff have suggested that biting should be considered a form of bullying. While biting is certainly a behavior that hurts the person who is bitten, toddler biting is quite different from bullying. As we see in chapter 1, there are many different reasons toddlers might bite. The biting happens as a result of one or more of these reasons. Here are several examples. A toddler who needs more oral motor stimulation might bite to get that stimulation. A toddler who is frustrated might bite to express and relieve that frustration. A toddler who is struggling to understand spatial relationships might bite when someone gets too close to them. When one toddler takes a toy away from another, that second child might bite out of sheer outrage and because he or she doesn't have the language to get it back. Biting, then, is a reactive behavior.

In contrast, bullying is an intentional behavior. The intention is to hurt or demean another person and to make the bully feel more powerful or to gain status. This requires intent and planning. The bully must consciously decide to act and must select a victim who is seen as weaker, more vulnerable, and unable to fight back.

Another difference is that even without intervention, most children who bit as toddlers do not bite when they are older. They don't need to bite because they are better able to regulate their emotions, to express themselves with language, and to solve problems with others. This comes with developmental maturation and life experience. We really don't find that biting is "unfortunately unexpected" among adults. On the other hand, without intervention, children who bully others intentionally may well continue this behavior as they get older, even into adulthood.

Program Perspectives on Biting

Whatever a program ultimately does about biting will be the result of the program staff's perspective on biting. Our perspectives reflect our beliefs, our attitudes, and our values. Our perspectives shape our goals, and our actions always flow from our goals.

Programs and providers who view biting only as a behavior problem will probably respond by disciplining the child. Their actions are likely to be punishments, which, as mentioned earlier, have been shown to be ineffective in stopping biting. Similarly, programs and providers who believe that toddlers bear all the responsibility for biting will respond by trying to fix the child. They will focus on getting the child to change and will not consider that their environment or practices may be a factor in the biting. On the other hand, programs and providers who believe that biting is inevitable will respond by "waiting out" the biting or hoping it won't get too bad. They may not take any action because they don't think they can do anything about it, since they believe biting is inevitable. Meanwhile, toddlers are injured, frightened, and confused, and parents are upset because biting continues and no one seems to know how to help or what to do.

If programs and providers want to be successful in dealing with biting, they must approach it in ways that are appropriate for children, families, and staff members. This is most likely to happen when they operate from a multidimensional perspective like this one:

We understand and accept that when toddlers are in groups, biting is unfortunately not unexpected.

We know and accept that toddlers bite for many reasons.

We believe that biting is never the right thing to do.

We want to help children who are bitten feel better by giving them care, support, and advice.

We want children who bite to learn and practice different, more appropriate behaviors.

We understand that our caregiving environment and practices can influence biting, and we take responsibility for ensuring they are appropriate for toddlers.

We understand that biting is very difficult for parents, and we communicate with them thoughtfully and frankly.

This perspective leads to two very worthwhile goals: to support toddlers whether they bite or are bitten and to support parents when biting occurs. With these goals in mind, you'll be less likely to look for the one perfect technique to implement, the one-size-fits-all plan for whenever biting occurs. Instead, as a professional you will approach each instance of biting from a problem-solving perspective. You will take into account developmental factors, treat each toddler as a unique individual, and look critically at the role of your caregiving environment in supporting or discouraging biting. That way you'll always have alternatives, unlike the people locked into their one "perfect" technique, who inevitably find themselves not knowing what to do when it doesn't work. You will be like a master craftsperson who designs a plan for each specific situation and carefully carries out that plan.

This book is based on that perspective, and we recommend it to you as you work to address the biting dilemmas in your program appropriately and effectively.

How to Use This Book

The book is organized into four main sections. Chapters 1, 2, and 3 address the problem itself: why toddlers bite, how to respond when they do, how to help both the child who is biting and the child who is being bitten, and how to develop a plan to deal with repeated biting. This part of the book will help you handle your foremost concern—the children.

Perhaps just as important in controlling biting is how you talk with parents and other caregivers. The second section, chapters 4 and 5, contains information on how parents see biting, how to talk with them about it, and how to respond to their suggestions and demands. It also addresses how biting affects adults other than parents—other staff members, even members of the larger community.

The third section, chapter 6, focuses on creating policies about biting. We know that programs and providers need to have policies in place *before* biting becomes a problem. To do this, policy makers need the information, experiences, and suggestions presented in the first two sections of the book to create policies that will work well for their program as well as for children, staff, and parents.

The fourth section, chapter 7, is designed for infant-toddler specialists who provide consultation and technical assistance on biting. It is a comprehensive guide to such consultation based on the principles and information in *No Biting*. It includes a perspective, a consulting process, examples from consultations with real toddler programs, and questions for reflection to help consultants build and strengthen skills.

The five appendixes contain sample letters, policies, forms, and staff development resources.

CHAPTER 1

Why Do Toddlers Bite?

Why *do* toddlers bite? It may be tempting to say, "I don't care *why* they bite; I just want them to stop." This reaction is certainly understandable, but it won't make the biting stop. Understanding why a toddler is biting is the first step to helping her stop. Often, nonetheless, adults insist, "She bit for no reason!" This reflects a view of toddler biting that is based on (and limited to) what makes sense and is apparent to the adult. Adults can understand that a toddler might bite when another child takes a toy away or hits. In the absence of such obvious reasons, however, many adults are baffled. They don't have the information or the understanding they need to work effectively with the toddler. Acknowledging that there is always a reason for the biting is important. Our role and responsibility is to identify the reason or reasons so we can work effectively with each child. The approach you take to help a child stop biting depends on knowing why she is biting in the first place.

Three Categories of Causes for Biting

Toddlers bite for many reasons, and these fall into three broad categories:

1. Developmental issues:

   - teething pain or discomfort

   - developing oral-motor skills

   - sensory exploration of the surroundings

   - learning about cause and effect

   - learning through imitating others

   - developing a sense of space

   - developing autonomy

   - developing expressive communication skills

- needing more attention

- learning to hold on and let go

- developing sensory integration

2. Expression of feelings:

- frustration

- anger

- tension

- anxiety

- excitement

- a reaction to abuse or other physical aggression

3. An environment or program that is not working for the child:

- an environment that is too stimulating or not stimulating enough

- a space that is too crowded and does not allow children privacy

- inappropriate expectations (such as expecting toddlers to share toys or equipment)

- a rigid schedule that does not meet toddlers' needs for food and sleep

Finding out why a particular toddler is biting requires thoughtful observation. Any one or a combination of the above reasons may be involved. These reasons are not a checklist that an adult can look at briefly to decide why a child is biting but rather a guide to many possibilities. It's possible to know what's going on with a particular child only by carefully watching him over time. On the following pages, we take a look at these broad categories to give you an idea of why a child might bite.

DEVELOPMENTAL REASONS FOR BITING

Understanding that many of the reasons for biting are related to development is important. It helps explain why we see so much biting in groups of toddlers but not in groups of preschoolers. It also puts biting into perspective: it points away from blaming toddlers for biting and toward understanding that while they are developing important knowledge and skills, biting is "not unexpected."

You are likely to notice that many of the developmental reasons for biting are interrelated. For example, toddlers are working on developing a sense of themselves as separate individuals with some power and control. At the same time, they often don't have the language skills to express themselves. Language skills are related to the development of oral-motor skills, which are necessary for speech. So a child may become frustrated when she feels powerless, such as when another child has a toy she wants. When she can't express herself verbally, she becomes even more frustrated. It may be the frustration that leads a child to bite, but the frustration is rooted in developmental considerations.

Teething. Some toddlers bite because of the pain and discomfort of teething. This is especially true of young toddlers, who may not make the distinction between a teething ring that feels good on sore gums and an arm that feels just as good. It is not usually difficult to recognize when a toddler is biting because of teething; she is most likely gnawing on just about everything.

Oral-Motor Skills. Another reason toddlers gnaw and may bite is because they are developing the oral-motor skills they need to speak and to eat without choking. At the toddler stage, this includes a great deal of chewing. They are exploring and experimenting with movement involving their mouths just as they do with other parts of their body. When toddler biting is related to developing oral-motor skills, we often see a great deal of oral-motor activity. Toddlers seek opportunities for oral stimulation: they put toys in their mouths and gum or chew them, they seek out activities that involve oral-motor skills, such as blowing bubbles, and they often prefer foods they can chew over softer foods.

Sensory Exploration. Toddlers may bite because they are exploring: they learn about objects and people using all their senses. This means they like to discover how things feel and taste in their mouths. It isn't too surprising when the exploration goes from mouthing to tasting to chomping. Observing this progression helps you know when a toddler is using biting as a way of exploring.

Cause and Effect. Toddlers may bite because they are learning about cause and effect: "What happens when . . . ?" This natural developmental curiosity may become, "What happens when I sink my teeth into Laura's arm?" A toddler who bites while he is learning about cause and effect usually does not appear to be upset before he bites. He also may look quite surprised when the child he is biting reacts loudly to being bitten.

Imitation. Toddlers may bite because they are imitating others. Toddlers use imitation as a way to learn. They learn many behaviors from other children, and biting can be one of them. Caregivers often report that after a period of time of no biting, one child bites, and the next thing they know, they have an epidemic. When this happens, children may well be biting in imitation of others. Toddlers might also imitate biting behaviors they learn from adoring, but unwitting, parents and grandparents. Who hasn't heard parents and grandparents look at infants and toddlers and proclaim, "You are just so wonderful I could eat you up"? The adult then follows this proclamation by pretending to nibble or gobble the wonderfully plump cheeks, tummy, or thighs of a delighted child. It is hardly surprising that toddlers try out the same behaviors. Unfortunately, they missed the part when the adults covered their teeth with their lips before chomping! When biting is related to this kind of imitation, we often see toddlers bite and then look to us with a big smile and an expression that seems to convey, "You are wonderful too. I could just eat you up!" Many caregivers find this is the situation when toddlers bite them.

Spatial Relationships. Toddlers may bite because they are developing an understanding of space and how it works. Toddlers are not able to judge a space or a distance by sight alone. To gain an understanding of space and spatial relationships, they must experiment physically, both with their own bodies and with materials—for example, by putting objects into containers and by trying to fit themselves into different spaces. With these kinds of experiments, they often end up on top of each other, and one child may become upset when another toddler gets too close. So biting can happen when children are too close together or when one child tries to get into the space already occupied by another. When biting is related to problems of physical closeness, a toddler may send a warning message by protesting when someone gets too close to him.

Autonomy. Toddlers may bite because of their developing understanding of autonomy. They are experimenting with asserting themselves as independent beings, and they are making choices and trying to control situations and other people. Some toddlers bite to demonstrate this control and to have power over others. It is quite easy to recognize when toddlers are trying to sort out autonomy—just listen for lots of "No!" "Mines!" and "Me do it!"

Language Limitations. Toddlers may bite because they don't have the language skills to express themselves. Because they are working on developing a sense of autonomy, they may have very definite ideas of what they want but not have the language to express those ideas. They don't have the words to convey their emotions, their needs, or their desires. It is very difficult for them to experience any control when other people do not understand what they want. The resulting frustration may cause them to express themselves by biting.

Attention. Toddlers may bite because they want and need more attention. Toddlers who need more attention than they are getting may notice that biting usually results in lots of attention. They would rather get the attention associated with biting—even if it is not pleasant—than get little or no attention. Recognizing that the need for attention belongs to the individual is very important. We may feel that a child is getting plenty of attention and doesn't need any more. Toddlers, however, do not base their desire for attention on what we think should be enough! If we purposefully withhold attention, toddlers may bite even more.

Holding On and Letting Go. Sometimes biting is related to maturation of the central nervous system, which allows toddlers to control the muscles that hold on and let go. At first the muscles that hold on are stronger than the muscles that let go. We see this in potty training, where toddlers learn to "hold it" until they get to the potty and then let go of the urine and feces. Toddlers are also working on emotional holding on and letting go. We see evidence of this in separation anxiety, when toddlers struggle with letting go of their parents. Biting can be evidence of learning to hold on and let go at another level. We see this when a toddler who might have been mouthing another child's arm suddenly finds that his teeth are holding on to the arm even though he didn't mean to bite. This is often frightening to both children.

Sensory Integration. Sensory integration is the ability to use our senses to take in, sort out, and connect information from the world around us in an organized way. When toddlers cannot organize the information they take in through their senses, it is difficult for them to respond with appropriate behavior. For example, toddlers who have problems with sensory integration may bite because they find ordinary movements frightening. They may end up biting someone when that was not what they meant to do. Children who need lots of sensory input may even bite themselves.

EXPRESSIVE REASONS FOR BITING

When it comes to self-expression, toddlers have not yet developed the range of skills and abilities that older children and adults have. Here are several examples. Toddlers can understand a great deal of what is said to them but have limited ability to express their own needs, wants, and ideas verbally. They are not yet able to regulate their own behavior and practice self-control. At the same time, they have definite ideas, and they know what they want. They experience strong emotions and need to express them in some way. Without being able to draw on language, self-regulation, and self-control, they often express themselves physically. Such physical expressions can include biting. Here are some reasons related to expressing emotions, ideas, needs, and wants that might explain why a particular toddler is biting.

Frustration. Toddlers may bite because they are frustrated. This frustration is sometimes related to their lack of language skills. Toddlers are working on language development, but when they know exactly what they want and don't yet have the words to make themselves understood, their frustration can mount and result in a chomp. Toddlers are just barely beginning to develop inner control, and when frustration becomes too great, they may bite.

Anger. Toddlers may bite to express their anger. When toddlers can't get people or objects to do what they want, they can easily become angry. Biting in this situation has been called an "oral tantrum." When toddlers bite out of frustration or anger, you can often see their frustration or anger building before the actual bite occurs.

Tension. Toddlers may bite to release tension. When people are under pressure, their bodies tend to become very tense. Toddlers may bite to relieve the tension in their mouths and jaws.

Anxiety. Toddlers may bite because they are feeling anxious. When toddlers are feeling insecure, scared, or confused about something at home or in the child care program, they may relieve the anxiety by biting. Many adults also use oral solutions to relieve anxiety—for example, smoking, eating, or drinking.

Excitement. Toddlers may bite because they are excited. Some toddlers get so excited they can't contain themselves. In the excitement of the moment, they just might joyously sink their teeth into a body part that is close to them. When one little boy seemed to be targeting a particular girl for biting, the staff at the center finally asked him, "Why do you bite Mary?" He jumped up and down, clapped his hands, and blurted out, "I just lub her!"

Self-Protection. Toddlers may bite as a reaction to a physical act that is happening to them. If a toddler is being abused, he may react by being physically aggressive, and this may include biting. If a child in group care is bitten many times, she may also begin to bite.

ENVIRONMENTAL REASONS FOR BITING

We are all aware that an environment can affect our mood and our behavior. For example, we feel and act differently in small settings with candlelight and soft music than in large arenas with blaring music, flashing lights, and a big crowd. The very same thing is true for toddlers. What is most important for them is that the classroom environment is a good match for their developmental needs. For example, we have seen that toddlers do not yet have a good sense of space; indeed, they often literally end up on top of each other. We also know that as they work on autonomy, an important developmental task, they are driven to explore. An environment that matches these developmental needs would have enough room to explore without constantly bumping into another explorer. That environment would also have enough interesting things to explore and time to thoroughly check them out. Here, then, are some reasons toddlers may bite that relate to the classroom environment.

Overstimulation. Toddlers may bite because they are overwhelmed by too much stimulation. There may be too many toys and materials; the environment may be too noisy; lights may be too bright; the schedule may be too rushed; there may not be enough time to relax. Toddlers become stressed, and stressed toddlers may bite.

Boredom. Toddlers may also bite because the program is not stimulating enough! They may become bored if they don't have enough toys, materials, or interaction with adults. Boredom is another kind of stress that leads to conflicts.

Overcrowding. Toddlers may bite because the space is too crowded and lacks enough private places to retreat to. Toddlers often find all kinds of small spaces to crawl into, but sometimes the room is arranged in such a way that all the children end up on top of each other. When children aren't able to find ways to remove themselves from the group, their frustration may result in biting.

Developmentally Inappropriate Expectations. Toddlers may bite when the program has inappropriate expectations—for example, if they are expected to share toys and there are no duplicates of popular or newly introduced toys. Toddlers usually have not reached a developmental level at which they can share toys or use them to play with other children.

Scheduling Issues. Toddlers may bite if the program schedule doesn't meet their needs. When toddlers must wait too long, when they become overtired or hungry, they are likely to bite. Because toddlers, like all people, have varying needs for food and sleep and different capacities for waiting, a flexible program that allows toddlers to eat and sleep on their own schedule is more likely to meet most of their needs most of the time than one that is rigid.

Preventing Biting

The lists in these three categories make it clear why, despite their best efforts, teachers cannot guarantee there won't be any biting in toddler programs. Toddlers bite for so many reasons that it is not possible to predict or prevent every bite. At the same time, children are more likely to bite when they are under stress or when their needs are not being met in the program. For this reason, teachers' expectations of children, interactions with children, and the program's physical environment and daily schedule can affect how likely children are to bite. This is especially true when one or two incidents of biting expand into a biting epidemic. When environments, schedules, expectations, and interactions don't match toddler development, we can expect to struggle with biting. Not only is biting more likely to occur, but it is also more difficult to respond to effectively. The rest of this chapter suggests things you can do to help prevent biting and make responding to a child who is biting easier.

PROVIDE A SUPPORTIVE ENVIRONMENT

▸ Have duplicates of new toys and popular toys to reduce frustration.

▸ Keep popular toys available, but avoid overstimulation by making sure all the toys aren't available to the children at once. Rotate toys: store some away for a while, then bring them back out and put others away.

▸ Provide enough of the kind of stimulation that is important to toddlers. This includes many positive, individual interactions with them.

▸ Provide small, private spaces where children can go to be alone. You still need to be able to see them, but they need to feel that they are alone. Toddlers are working on understanding spatial relationships; that's why they like to try fitting themselves into small spaces.

▸ Provide several soft areas in the room. Use pillows, rugs, and comfortable upholstered furniture to provide coziness.

▸ Have safe materials visible and available at the children's level so they can use them without adult assistance.

▸ Create a variety of activity centers to discourage toddlers from bunching up in one area. Staff should spread themselves throughout the space; children often want to be where the adults are.

▸ Keep some of the activity areas and materials that toddlers find most interesting available throughout the day.

▸ Provide a menu that includes foods toddlers can gum, munch, and chew. Examples include banana chunks, soft tortilla strips, bagel pieces, and soft raw vegetables, such as zucchini, lettuce, and spinach leaves.

PROVIDE A CONSISTENT YET FLEXIBLE SCHEDULE

▸ Keep the daily schedule consistent so that it is predictable for children. Being able to predict what comes next is empowering.

▸ Simplify the daily routine and allow for flexibility to meet children's individual needs. Children need to eat when they are hungry and sleep when they are tired, regardless of whether it's snack or naptime.

▸ Talk with the children about unavoidable changes in the schedule, and be understanding of their reactions.

▸ Provide several opportunities each day for children to go outside.

▸ Keep waiting time to a minimum. Most teachers believe that waiting times in their program are very short, and they are surprised when they learn how long toddlers actually wait between activities. Try asking an objective person to observe your program and keep track of actual waiting time in minutes. To put the waiting time into perspective, take the number of minutes toddlers must wait, multiply by ten, and reflect on how you would react to that waiting time in that situation. For example, if the actual waiting time between the end of an activity and lunch is seven minutes, consider how you would respond to a seventy-minute wait in a similar situation. And remember: you would be expected to be still, be quiet, and be good during those seventy minutes.

▸ Take the time to go through the daily routine calmly, and don't rush children through activities or routines. This includes naptime. It is very unfair to toddlers to wake them up while they are sound asleep simply because afternoon snack is at one thirty.

PROVIDE A VARIETY OF SENSORY ACTIVITIES AND MATERIALS

▸ Provide a wide variety of soothing materials and activities, such as scarves and dress-up clothes that are soft and silky and cleaned often. Have sensory activities like painting and working with playdough available every day. The sand and water table should be available to toddlers at least several times a week. If your program doesn't have a sand and water table, you can use small individual basins.

▸ Provide activities and materials for oral stimulation and for practicing oral-motor skills. Examples include bubbles and musical instruments that make sounds when blown into.

▸ Provide many cause-and-effect toys that toddlers can act on to make them "do something." Musical instruments, busy boxes, pounding boards, and jack-in-the-boxes are all examples of cause-and-effect toys.

▸ Provide opportunities for toddlers to put collections of small, choking-safe objects (for example, clothespins, jar lids, juice can lids) in containers, carry them around, and then dump them out. This is a favorite toddler activity and, if indulged, soon progresses to the point at which they can begin to learn about picking up.

▶ Instead of planning teacher-directed activities, offer interesting materials and experiences. Observe the children's reactions to the materials, and then plan how to further their interest. Offer the same thing over and over so that children have many opportunities to experiment.

▶ Offer adult-initiated activities that are spontaneous, short, and optional, such as songs, stories, and fingerplays.

▶ Do not expect toddlers to have formal circle time or to sit throughout whole-group activities.

INTERACT WITH CHILDREN GENTLY AND EMPATHETICALLY

▶ Show children what empathy looks like and sounds like; model it in your interactions with them.

▶ Respond positively to children.

▶ Help children identify and name their feelings. Say things such as, "Ramon, you look sad to me. Are you feeling sad right now?" or "Robin, you look frustrated to me. You really wanted to play with that truck, and Sonja has it."

▶ Show and tell children how to use language to express feelings and state their needs and wants. Say things such as, "Robin, you can tell Sonja, 'My turn next.' That way she knows you're waiting for the truck."

▶ Encourage children to comfort themselves by using transitional items like stuffed animals or blankets brought from home or by sucking their thumb or pacifier (if that is what they already do to comfort themselves).

▶ Comfort children with soothing voice tone and physical actions, such as hugs, gentle hands on their shoulders, and back rubs.

▶ Help children fix mistakes. For example, if a child looks genuinely upset that she hurt another, you can say, "Sammy, you look upset that Lonetta is crying. I wonder if she'd like a hug?" Other possible ways to fix a mistake include helping rebuild a knocked-down tower, kissing a "boo-boo," fetching ice for a bite, and saying you're sorry (do not impose apologies; they should come from a child's own feelings and not be an adult-imposed formula).

▶ Give attention in a generous and genuine manner.

Despite the best efforts of the best caregivers to prevent it, biting still (unfortunately) happens. When it does occur, toddler caregivers must be prepared to respond appropriately and effectively. The next chapter shows you how.

CHAPTER 2

What to Do When Toddlers Bite

What most caregivers want to know is, "What do I *do* when a toddler bites?" Unfortunately, there is no simple answer. As the introduction noted, because toddlers bite for a variety of reasons and in a variety of circumstances, there is no one-size-fits-all response to biting. The response that helps a child stop biting and keeps other children safe is different depending on each child's needs, temperament, and reason for biting.

To determine the best response in a given situation, teachers must observe the child closely to find out why he is biting. While gathering this information, pay attention to the environmental factors that might be encouraging the biting, and try to prevent as many further bites as possible. The next chapter will tell you what to do when you have a pattern of ongoing biting in your program or when the same child bites repeatedly. This chapter focuses on what to do in the moment after a child has been bitten. The immediate response should always be the same, whether it's the first time the child has bitten or his seventh bite that day.

Whenever you're dealing with biting, you need to act quickly and directly. You want your words, attitudes, and actions to convey a strong message:

▸ Biting is not the right thing to do.

▸ You will help the child who was bitten feel better.

▸ You will help the child who bit learn and practice different, more appropriate behavior.

When you are responding to individual biting incidents, you probably won't see the actual bite—only the aftermath. Nevertheless, by looking at the two children, you can usually get some idea of the circumstances. For example, children who bite because they are exploring, mouthing, or experimenting with cause and effect may look rather surprised at the outraged cries of their victims. When children bite out of frustration or anger, you may see evidence of their feelings in their voices, facial expressions, or body language. If you see one child triumphantly holding a toy while another child with bite marks on her arm is crying and pointing to the toy, you have a pretty good idea of what happened.

At this point, you have to decide where to go and what to say. On some occasions, you will want to separate the children; at other times you will want the children to be near each other while you deal with the biting. Separate the children when emotions are still high and you worry that more biting will take place if the children remain near each other. Pay attention to the feelings of the child who was bitten:

- ▶ If she is scared or worried, separate her from the child who bit her, even if it's just positioning yourself between the two children.

- ▶ If she is furious and ready to retaliate, separate the children to prevent escalation.

- ▶ If she is indignant, you might bring both children together so the victim can express her outrage directly.

You can also use the reaction of the child who bit to help decide whether to separate the children. If he is calm, curious, or content after biting, it may be a good idea to have him nearby to see the negative effects of his biting.

If you decide to separate the children, either you must have two caregivers who can each attend to one child or one caregiver must attend to both children, one at a time. If you are attending to both children, you must decide whom to go to first. Unless the child who bit is in danger of hurting someone else, go to the child who was bitten first. Meanwhile, make sure the child who bit sees the aftermath of the biting as you tend to the child who was bitten. Without being punitive, tell the child who bit, "Stay right here for a minute." The more neutral you can be, the better—it's important that you not be angry or show other emotions. You're not giving him a time-out or punishing him in some way; you just want him to wait so you can finish interacting with him after you've cared for the child who was bitten.

Helping the Child Who Was Bitten

Check the bite and give the appropriate first aid (see pages 21–22 for first aid information). Comfort the child. Let the child know that you sincerely regret he was bitten, that it wasn't right. This can be a simple statement, such as "I'm sorry you got hurt" or "Maeko bit you, and that's not right." It is important for the child to hear this message. It affirms for the child that this is not something that should happen to him. The child may protest the bite in a manner that reflects his expressive language limitations. He may cry, jabber indignantly, or protest with words, phrases, or short sentences. Respond to these by acknowledging his feelings and letting him know he has every reason to protest. "You are right! That really hurt, and no one should bite you!" This helps children know they have been heard and understood.

You can also tell the child what he can do to respond to the child who bit him. You shouldn't insist that he do it, but you can help the child understand that a response is possible and give him the language and the confidence to respond appropriately. This can be a short statement like, "You can tell Maeko no." You can also give the child advice about what to do if he is worried someone might be about to bite him. Tell the child, "If you're worried someone will hurt you, you can say, 'Stop!' or 'No!'" Teach the child to deliver this message in an emphatic tone of voice.

You can also teach him some effective body language. Show the child how to put his hand up, palm out, at arm's length in front of him while he says, "Stop!" Doing so helps prevent anyone coming toward him to bite from getting to the softer, fleshier parts that are easier to bite. Instead, the biter will encounter the palm of his hand, which is harder to bite. This is a powerful suggestion for the child who has been bitten. He doesn't have to wait until after he's been bitten to act. He doesn't have to guess whether the other child might bite him; he can act on his own feelings. Having an appropriate way to act on our feelings is empowering for all of us. This suggestion can also help prevent some bites. It may prevent a child from getting close enough to bite and give you time to intervene. When a child tries this behavior, go to him and let him know he is doing it correctly. "Good for you. You were worried she might hurt you, and you said, 'Stop.' That's exactly right." You can further reinforce this by telling the child who may have been about to bite, "He just said 'Stop!' and I have to say, it looks like he means it! Let's find something else for you to do."

Finally, take your cue from the child to decide what other steps may be needed to help him. He may want to stay close to you for a while, he may want to be near other children, or he may want to play alone in a quiet space.

FIRST AID FOR BITES

The Task Force on Biting contacted Dr. Gary Johnson, currently chair of emergency medicine at Upstate University Hospital in Syracuse, New York, for information on treating bites in child care settings. Dr. Johnson reviewed and confirmed his original advice for this edition. He advises that if the skin is not broken, you don't have to worry about infection. However, the bite may still hurt quite a bit, and you may want to offer to put ice on it. Some programs keep ice in small packs or "boo-boo bunnies" (washcloths folded to look like a bunny with a pouch for an ice cube) available for such use. Other programs use frozen sponges; wet paper towels in small, sealed plastic bags; frozen teething rings; or bags of frozen vegetables. The frozen vegetables seem to be very popular because they can be molded to shapes of various body parts!

If the skin is broken, you need to clean the wound. First, wash your own hands thoroughly. If the wound is bleeding, apply direct pressure to stop the bleeding. Then clean the wound with soap and water. Antibiotic creams and ointments can help prevent infections. (Note: Child care program regulations vary from state to state. Check your state's regulations and your program's policies on the use of over-the-counter ointments before using them.) After the wound is cleaned, exposure to open air is optimal. If the wound is bleeding or if the child is likely to get dirt in it, cover it with a bandage.

You need to be especially concerned with bites that break the skin on the top of the hand and on the fingers because bacteria may come into contact with tendons. Dr. Johnson recommends that when such bites occur, children should be seen by medical personnel.

The issue of biting can be further inflamed when adults call the human mouth "the filthiest of all mouths." This language is especially upsetting because we usually think of biting as an animal, not a human, behavior. According to the article "Human Bites: First Aid" on the Mayo Clinic's website, human bites "can be as dangerous or even more dangerous" than the bites of animals because of the "types of bacteria and viruses contained in the human mouth." This information seems to support the view that children who bite are indeed dangerous. However, there are many other ways that young children in group care spread bacteria and viruses to others, and we typically do not think of those ways as dangerous. We can best use this information to talk about the issue accurately and to focus on the importance of appropriate first aid for bites.

Helping the Child Who Bit

Once the child who was bitten is calm, you can turn to the child who bit. A toddler's attention span is usually quite short, so you want to do this within a minute or two. When you respond to the child who bit, be genuine, brief, and serious. Respond verbally and with an action, even when the action is something as simple as redirecting the child.

Your verbal response must clearly indicate that biting is not the right thing to do. This is not a time to laugh, snicker, or use any kind of humor. You don't want the child to get the impression that biting is cute or funny. Use a genuine tone of voice that sounds serious without being threatening. This is especially important because toddlers may not understand all your words, but they will understand the tone of your voice, and that's what they will respond to. You can use serious words, but if your tone of voice is light and friendly, you are not sending a serious message. Many caregivers find that lowering both the pitch and the volume of their voice slightly while speaking firmly conveys a sense of seriousness. It's important to state briefly and clearly what happened and that the biting was not okay. This is especially helpful for toddlers because it enhances the language skills they are struggling to develop. Here are some examples of possible things to say to a child who has just bitten another child:

▶ "You bit him with your teeth. He doesn't like it. It's not okay to bite people." (By adding the words "with your teeth," this response clarifies the word *bit* for very young toddlers.)

▶ "You bit her, and it hurt her. That's why she's crying. I don't want you to bite anyone."

▶ "You were so mad when the truck wouldn't work! And you bit Trey. Biting hurts people. I'll help you when you're mad, but you may not bite people."

▶ "Emily had a toy you wanted, and you bit her to take it away. Biting hurts people, and you can't have toys when you bite people to get them."

▶ "You bit Ryan and hurt him. He was trying to get into your cubby with you. You can tell him, 'No, Ryan!' But there is no biting."

▶ "Oh dear. You were trying to kiss Lee, but you hurt him with your teeth. Please be careful so you don't bite people."

Note that these responses are all very specific in describing what happened and why biting is not okay. They are different from "That's not nice," a response we often hear from caregivers. While indeed biting is not nice, such a response is too vague. It doesn't convey the understanding that biting is the wrong thing to do. Notice, too, that none of these responses refers to hurting "our friends." Rather, they refer to the child who was bitten by name. This makes it much more personal and specific. The children in a child care program are not necessarily all friends, nor do they need to be. When we use phrases such as "We don't bite our friends," the underlying message is that while we don't bite people who are identified as our friends, other people are fair game!

Avoid using verbal responses that are outrageous, untrue, or frightening for toddlers. Telling a toddler that all her teeth will fall out if she bites, for example, is both unfair to the child (because it is untrue) and ineffective in stopping the biting.

TIE YOUR VERBAL RESPONSE TO AN ACTION RESPONSE

The verbal response should almost always be followed by an action response. The action you choose to take must fit the circumstances of the incident, but it may also include advice and actions for the child to try. As we have seen, biting is not usually an intentional act. It often occurs when toddlers have trouble with what they are trying to accomplish. While we want to send the message that biting is not the right thing to do, we also need to direct toddlers to what we *do* want them to do.

If you take a moment to try to understand what the toddler was thinking, you can gain insight that will help you give her advice. Here's an example. Suppose Anna is playing with a shape sorter. She tries and tries to get the square shape into the round hole. She pounds harder and harder. Malik toddles over to her and reaches for the shape sorter, and Anna bites him on the arm. Suppose you deal effectively with both Malik and Anna as described earlier in this chapter. You can take an additional action step that will be very helpful to Anna. If you consider this situation, you realize that Anna thought she would be able to get the square shape into the round hole. She tried it, but it didn't work. So she tried a different strategy—she pounded harder. That didn't work either. Her frustration was building, and she eventually bit. If you were to give Anna some advice about the shape sorter, you could help her develop skills to prevent frustration. "Anna, here's what I know about the shape sorter. When one piece doesn't fit, maybe another piece will." You can then spend a few minutes with Anna and the shape sorter, helping her use your advice to experiment and problem solve. In this instance, you have crafted a response that not only addresses the behavior but also helps the child learn a new strategy to solve a problem and avoid frustration.

If the biting was a matter of mouthing or exploration, a caregiver can demonstrate how to touch without hurting. Use gentle or other appropriate touches on the child who just bit and, in some cases, on the child who was bitten. Don't insist that the child who bit try out the gentle touches on the child who was just bitten. The timing may not be right. Be sure to include lots of language with your demonstrations. Here are some examples:

▶ "I'm going to use my fingers to touch your arm. Your arm feels smooth and warm. I don't use my teeth on your arm."

▶ "You can use your hand to touch Juan's cheek if he wants you to."

▶ "I'll touch your hand like this so you will know how to touch Libby's hand."

When a child's biting is related to anger, a caregiver can help him learn the words, tone of voice, and body language to express anger in a powerful but safe manner. Depending on the child's language ability, teach him to say phrases such as, "Oh no!" or "I'm so mad!" or "The truck wouldn't work right!" in an emphatic tone of voice. Show him how to add emphatic body language by putting his hands on his hips or crossing his arms over his chest with great gusto. When you see and hear him use such expressions, tone, and body language to express anger, let him know, "That's exactly the way to do it. I could tell that you were really mad. Good for you."

Sometimes a toddler caregiver has the child who bit help care for the child who was just bitten. This typically involves getting a wet cloth or holding a frozen sponge on the bite for the other child. While this can be very effective for both children, you need to take your cue from the children, particularly the child who was bitten. It should be up to the child who was bitten to accept or refuse the help; this gives her at least a small measure of control, which is important after not being able to control being bitten. The child who bit may also balk or refuse to help take care of the bite he just inflicted. Insisting that a child in these circumstances must help take care of the other child is not likely to be very effective. In addition, it isn't very reassuring or comforting to the child who was just bitten to find that she is going to be taken care of by someone who is resistant or belligerent.

APOLOGIES

Should we ever require the child who bit to apologize? Many caregivers try to have older toddlers say "I'm sorry" to the children they bit. The thought behind this practice is to teach children to be accountable for their behavior by apologizing. While this may be a good motive, the practice is not a good fit for toddlers or for biting. When older toddlers are reminded or forced to say "I'm sorry" in situations in which their behavior was inappropriate, they can readily learn to utter the words. They can even learn the correct contrite tone of voice. It does not guarantee, however, that they feel remorse for hurting someone else or that they are consciously taking responsibility for their behavior. Some older toddlers will dutifully say "I'm sorry" and turn right around and bite again. When this happens, caregivers and parents might interpret it to mean that the child knows biting is wrong and bites anyway. They may view the child as biting intentionally, with premeditated malice. This interpretation is likely to result in very ineffective responses from adults that focus on punishing the child rather than teaching him other ways of expressing himself or dealing with his emotions.

When a child utters the required words of apology, adults consider the matter settled and do not spend any time working on helping the child learn different behavior or considering changes that should be made to the environment to help reduce biting. Over time children learn that it's all right to hurt other people as long as they say "I'm sorry" afterward. Adults don't intend for this to be the lesson children learn, but often it is. Ironically, it's also the very opposite of genuinely taking responsibility for their own behavior.

REDIRECTION

Another good action to take after responding verbally to a child who bit is to use redirection—directing a toddler's attention to a different toy, activity, person, or area of the room. Redirection is most likely to work well when it is specific. Telling a toddler, "You need to find something else to do," doesn't work nearly as well as "This doll needs a ride in the buggy" or "I see Rhonda getting the fingerpaints out." Fortunately, most toddlers are easily redirected.

In some cases, toddlers may insist on doing what you're pretty sure is going to lead to another bite or continuing to do what led to the bite in the first place. When you try to redirect them, they may be resistant. You may want to combine several strategies. For example, you can

- ▸ acknowledge their feelings (and the depth of their feelings); say something such as, "You really want to hug Jessie, but she doesn't want you to hug her right now," or "You really want to be in that cubby, but Tyrone is in there right now."

- ▸ redirect them; say something such as, "I wonder if Sydney would like a hug instead," or "Tyrone's in the cubby, but I see an empty place under the loft," or "Carmen has the blue ball, but I see a big red ball on the floor."

- ▸ give them choices; say something such as, "You could see if Sydney wants a hug, or give me a big hug," or "You could go in that empty space under the loft or try fingerpainting with Rhonda," or "You could play with the big red ball or play at the water table with Niki."

Here is an example of how it might work when you put all three redirection strategies together: "You wish you could stay here and get into the cubby with Tyrone. But only one person can be in the cubby at a time. You can go in a different cubby, or you can play with the trucks."

These responses help children who have just bitten understand that biting is not the right thing to do and that you will help them learn different, more appropriate behavior.

A child should never profit by biting. If a child bites to get a toy away from another child, he should not be allowed to keep the toy. Even if the other child quickly forgets about the toy, taking the toy away helps send the message that biting is not the right thing to do. This also helps toddlers learn about cause and effect.

What Not to Do

Because biting is such a problem in toddler programs, adults are always looking for and are willing to try almost any suggestion to deal with it. They often try techniques that they have heard about (but not really thought about) only to discover that they're not very effective. This is frustrating for everyone and often leads to claims such as "We've tried everything, and nothing works!" Here are some of those failed techniques along with explanations about why they are ineffective.

TIME-OUT

One technique that is often suggested or tried with young children in programs is time-out. Not being allowed to participate in an activity may make sense to adults as a punishment, and it might even serve to eliminate an older child's misbehavior. A time-out makes sense to us as adults because we can connect the punishment to the behavior. Toddlers, however, do not experience a time-out in the same way because they don't make that connection. As developmental psychologist Jean Piaget reminds us, the way young children think and reason is different from the way older children and adults think and reason.

Trying to put a toddler in a time-out after biting may be as frustrating for the adult as it is for the child. The toddler can't figure out why the adult is so insistent that she sit, and the adult can't figure out why the toddler won't stay in time-out. The end result is a battle between the adult and the toddler.

Some adults believe time-out offers an opportunity for children to think about what they did. Can any of us really imagine toddlers who have bitten thinking to themselves, "Oh dear. I was frustrated because I don't have the language to express my feelings. I took it out on another child by biting. I hurt this other child, and now I feel very sorry for doing it. I should not do this and will never do it again"?

Caregivers may still protest that a toddler "knows what she's doing is wrong because whenever she bites she goes over and sits in the time-out chair." This was observed in one program in which a child of twenty months had been biting. The caregivers had been using time-outs with this child and were frustrated because while time-outs "seemed to be working," the little girl was still biting. During the observation, the little girl was tussling over a toy with another toddler, a boy of about the same age and size. After a brief struggle, the little girl bit the boy, who promptly let go of the toy. The little girl then took herself to the time-out chair, where she sat playing with the very toy she had bitten to get. After a few moments, she got up and returned to the group, still playing with the toy. The caregiver was convinced that the girl realized that biting was bad because she went to the time-out chair voluntarily. The caregiver was frustrated because even though the child had "served time" for her "crime," she was still biting.

To the outside observer, it was obvious that the girl had learned that biting was followed by a short sit-down period. Putting herself in a time-out had nothing to do with knowing or caring that she had hurt another child. Rather, time-outs had become part of the biting routine. And we know that routines are very important and powerful to toddlers.

SAYING, "HOW WOULD YOU LIKE IT . . . ?"

Sometimes when toddlers bite, adults say to them, "How would you like it if he bit you?" Variations of this technique include "Would you want someone to bite you?" and "Do you like it when people bite you?"

If they respond to these questions at all, most toddlers will say, "No." And truly, they wouldn't want someone to bite them, and they don't like it when people bite them.

Having gotten toddlers to agree that they wouldn't want to be bitten, adults then take the next logical step, which is to say, "Well, then, if you would not want to be bitten, probably the child you just bit didn't want to be bitten either." This makes sense to adults because it is the next logical step. And this is exactly why it doesn't work with toddlers. They don't make that logical step because they don't think logically. Logic is one of the characteristics of the thinking of older children and adults, not of young children.

So if you get a toddler to agree that he would not want to be bitten, you really can't expect him to make the connection to not biting another child. And because he doesn't make that connection, your saying, "Would you like it if . . . ?" is not very effective in stopping him from biting.

LECTURING OR GOING ON A TIRADE

Sometimes adults respond to biting by telling the child at length what she did wrong and why (a lecture) or by telling her over and over again, with a lot of emotion, not to do something (a tirade). These are both ineffective in stopping biting behavior. Adults may lecture or go off on tirades because it makes them feel as if they are doing something about the biting. It can also release the tension they may feel about the biting incident. (Ironically, toddlers may also be trying to relieve tension by biting. A tirade might be thought of as an adult version of biting!)

Lectures are ineffective because they are usually too long and not given in toddler-friendly language. Children lose track of what an adult is talking about very quickly, especially in an emotional situation. They need to hear briefly and clearly what happened, what was wrong, and what to do next.

Tirades are ineffective because the adult's voice and body language frighten or surprise children, and the message usually gets lost. Remember: adding to children's stress increases the chance they will bite someone. In some tirades, the word "bite" or "biting" is used so often and with such emphasis that it might actually sound like a cheer urging on children to bite. Here's an example:

"You just bit her. There is no biting here. Biting is very bad. Biting hurts other people. We don't bite. Do you want someone to bite you? Don't bite! Don't bite! Don't bite! Do you hear me? Do not bite!"

Delivered in a loud, passionate voice, a tirade can be intense enough to make anyone—especially a toddler—feel like chomping something. Adults need to be aware that just because they feel better after they have delivered a lecture or tirade doesn't mean that they have affected the biting at all.

USING AUTOMATIC COMMENTS

Early childhood teachers are always looking for ways to respond effectively to children. Often when they encounter phrases that they decide "sound good," they begin using them without really thinking them through. A current example is addressing unwanted behaviors by telling a child, "No, thank you." Teachers may feel that they have effectively told the child no without sounding harsh. Sometimes they add a phrase to indicate to the child what behavior they are referring to. Here is a real-life example from a classroom I visited: "No, thank you for smacking your friend in the head."

If we really think this through, we realize that this message doesn't fit the way "No, thank you" is used in our language. It is usually a response to a question. "Would you like more milk?" "No, thank you." When an adult uses "No, thank you" as a stand-alone comment, there is no context, and it doesn't fit the pattern. That makes it difficult for children to figure out what it's supposed to mean.

If a teacher does add context, such as "No, thank you for biting your friend," it still doesn't make sense, and it's confusing. Children are figuring out that usually "No, thank you" indicates that something is appreciated but not wanted just now. So this phrase actually sends the message that "I appreciate your biting your friend, but just not right now." And, of course, that's not what the teacher means to convey at all. By saying, "No, thank you," teachers may feel that they have sent a good message, but this comment rarely gets the desired result.

These types of comments are ineffective for yet another reason. They can easily become so automatic that teachers deliver them from across the room or as they walk past children without even making eye contact. We can think of them as drive-by comments. They don't come across as important, and children hear them so often that they learn to tune them out. Even positive comments can become so automatic that they lose the power to be effective.

When it comes to biting, I have heard, "Not safe, not safe." "We bite food, not friends." "Teeth are for food, not friends." While true, these phrases can start to replace responses that are specific to the child and the situation. It's not that they are so terrible; it's that they crowd out personal interactions and responses that we know are much more effective.

CHAPTER 3

Handling Ongoing Biting

Isolated biting incidents are difficult enough. Many caregivers feel overwhelmed when the biting becomes repeated, involves more than one child, or seems to go on and on. When you are faced with patterns of biting, you need to develop a plan that involves observation and reflection and uses specific strategies and techniques. These strategies and techniques should be identified and chosen because they are a good match for the patterns and situations you are facing. This chapter will help you develop a plan to cope with ongoing biting and carry it out step-by-step. It addresses situations in which more than one child may be biting as well as those in which the same child bites repeatedly.

To make a plan, you need to gather some information by

1. observing the children who are biting,

2. consulting with the parents of the children who are biting, and

3. observing and reflecting on your program.

These three steps will help you gain insight into the biting. Without taking all of these steps, you will not be able to tailor your approach to the needs of the children who are biting, and that makes your plan less likely to succeed. Once you have gathered thorough information, you will be able to assess the problem and develop a comprehensive plan to address it.

Observe the Child

Note: The term child *is used in this section, but the information applies whether several different children are biting or one child is biting repeatedly. The next section discusses additional considerations when you have one child who bites again and again.*

Remember that long list of reasons why children bite in chapter 1? Observing the child as soon as you realize you have a biting problem in your program is the first step toward understanding why the child is biting. You need observations that will yield information about the biting incidents and information about the child's personality, development, interests, and style of interacting with the environment. Information about the biting incidents will help you discover patterns. Information about the child will show you how the child interacts with teachers, other children, and the environment. You will need to keep track of the following information for at least a week in order to have enough details about the child to make a good guess about what is going on.

Do the bites always happen at the same time of the day? (Maybe the child is hungry or tired at that time, or maybe it's an especially chaotic time in your schedule.) Do the bites happen at different times of the day but always during a transition? (Maybe transitions are especially hard for the child.) Do the bites always happen in one part of the room? (Maybe that part of the room is drawing too many children, or there's a bottleneck there that's leading to frustration.) These, and many other possibilities, will be revealed as you keep track of what actually happens when the child bites. If more than one child is biting, you'll need to keep careful observations about each one.

Whenever a bite occurs, you need to fill out an incident report, which contains some of the information listed below. Your observations of the child, however, must go beyond the immediate facts of the incident itself. Taken together, the incident reports and the observations of the child should include the following:

- ▶ when the bites have taken place
- ▶ where in the environment the bites have taken place
- ▶ whom the child has bitten
- ▶ what was happening just before each bite
- ▶ the child's reaction after biting
- ▶ the child's social interaction skills
- ▶ the child's oral-motor skills
- ▶ the child's motor skills
- ▶ the child's general personality characteristics
- ▶ the child's chronological age

As you complete your observations, review them to see if you can find any patterns. Biting is rarely a random event; a child almost always bites for a reason. You may be able to find several patterns, perhaps one having to do with the time of the bites, another having to do with who is being bitten, or another having to do with where the child is in the room when she bites. Two examples of actual observations appear in appendix B. They were made during the course of typical mornings in child care settings. Each one contains observations, reflections, and insights into the child's biting and includes related recommendations to help reduce the biting. The Biting Incident Documentation and Reflection Form and the accompanying guide in appendix C is an excellent resource to record both information and insights into a child's biting. This form is very helpful in thinking about the biting by focusing on the specific child and why he or she may be biting. This gives you a solid foundation for creating an appropriate plan to address the biting.

Be sure to notice any times or places in which biting does not occur. Often, for instance, caregivers discover that biting does not happen outside, perhaps because children have more space.

SPECIAL CONSIDERATIONS WHEN ONE CHILD BITES REPEATEDLY

One of the most challenging situations in toddler care occurs when one child bites again and again. This is when it is especially important to focus on positive ways to help the child learn to stop biting. A very common and seemingly innocent practice often gets in the way: referring to the toddler who bites repeatedly as "the biter." Many caregivers insist that since the child *is* biting, it is fitting to refer to her as the biter. There is a great deal of difference, however, between the way we think about a child who is biting and a child who is a biter. Since our thoughts guide our actions, it is worth looking at this more closely.

It is unfair to the child to be labeled a biter or—even worse—*the* biter. First, any label serves to define a child and shapes the way adults respond to and interact with her. The label *biter* portrays a child in a negative light and is likely to result in responses from adults that are less supportive and more negative—even if the adult is unaware of it. Second, the label is based on only one behavior—biting. We don't use such labels for other behaviors. A toddler who has frequent bowel movements is not called "the pooper." We don't refer to a child who often tips over her juice cup as "the spiller." Besides being unfair, labeling a child as a biter gets in the way of effective practices because it suggests that there may be little we, the adults, can do about the biting. It directs our attention toward blaming the child and away from considering how to help the child learn not to bite. It also diverts our attention away from considering that some of our own practices and behaviors may be contributing to the biting. When a child is biting repeatedly, refer to her by name. Insist that others do the same, and explain why. It seems like a small thing, but it really does matter.

When the same child bites repeatedly, adult frustrations often run very high. This is true of both parents and caregivers. Because the pressure is on, caregivers frequently respond by trying one technique after another with little thought given to whether any of them match the specific child and situation. Techniques are tried for a day or two and then replaced by others. When the biting continues, adults often throw up their hands, declaring, "We've tried everything, and nothing works." The implication is clear: since everything has been tried, nothing more can be done and nothing more can be expected. This is when programs and staff feel justified in expelling a child.

To address this difficult situation, you need a plan that has been carefully and thoughtfully crafted to be appropriate for the child. Such a plan is based on careful observations of the child *in the child care environment* and on thoughtful reflection about how what you observe relates to biting. From there it is not difficult to craft a plan that is likely to be very effective.

Consult with the Parents

While you are gathering information about the child's biting, you will need to talk with her parents. From the incident reports, the parents will already know that their child has been biting, but you will want to tell them what you have noticed in your program and ask them what (if anything) they have noticed at home. Ask them if they have any insights into the biting or if they are aware of anything their child seems upset or worried about. Allow time and opportunity for parents to ask you questions too. You can tell them that you are keeping track of the biting to try to understand its pattern and that when you have enough information, you will be making a plan to address the biting. They will probably want to know how you handle the child after she bites, and they will probably need to be reassured that their child really is okay, not a monster! (See chapter 4 for more information about talking with parents.)

Reflect on the Program

Before you make a plan, you need to observe your program to find out how well it's working for the children, and particularly for the child who is biting. In what ways might your program be contributing to the biting? Examine your environment, materials, activities, schedule, and interactions with children. You can use the preventive measures mentioned on pages 15–18 as a checklist to complete this observation and reflection. You might ask your administrator to come in and observe as well.

Objective observation can be extremely difficult. In one program, teachers were frustrated when technique after technique failed to make a dent in the biting, which involved several children. Finally, an outside observer asked if there were any times at all during the day when there was no biting. At first the staff answered that there wasn't, but as they went through the daily schedule, they realized the biting did not occur when the children went outside. The teachers changed the schedule temporarily to go outdoors with the children three times during the day instead of just once. It was a big adjustment, but the biting stopped. The teachers then went on to look at the difference between the classroom and the outdoor environment. They realized that the classroom was very crowded and children were tripping over each other. They tried changing the room arrangement so children had more space to move about without getting in one another's way. With these changes, the biting stopped even when the children were inside.

Objective observation means being brutally honest with yourself, because the program has such a huge impact on the children. A biting problem can almost always be helped by a change in the program. If, for example, you rarely offer activities or materials such as sand and water play or painting because they are too messy, you are probably not providing adequate sensory experiences for the children. Sensory play is one of the most effective tools for preventing biting, and providing many opportunities for sensory play can have a huge impact on biting. If you don't like to offer sand and water play, find someone who can help increase your comfort level with this activity. As you discover ways to keep the mess minimal or easy to clean up, you may be less likely to limit the children's experiences. You will need every tool you can find to help the biting stop, and it's much easier to ask children and families to change their behavior when you yourself have been willing to make changes.

Develop a Plan

From your observations of the children and your conferences with parents, you can determine a possible reason or reasons the child may be biting. Your observation and reflection on your program will help you identify specific areas that may be contributing to the biting. Use the information you have gathered in these three steps to develop an action plan. Write down what specifically you are going to do to change your program and what specific strategies you are going to use with the child. Make sure the expectations of the child are reasonable. Consider planning in small steps so the child can be successful and build skills. Careful planning that focuses on all aspects of the child's development will result in a plan that is supportive and will focus on building replacement skills the child can use instead of biting. If the steps can be easily introduced at home, this can also be part of the plan. It further supports the child by creating consistency between the messages and expectations at home and those in your program. Check with parents, and if they are willing, write it into the plan.

Write down the timeline and who is responsible for each part of the plan. For example, "We need more sensory experiences. The water table will be available every day. Janine will supervise it."

To address ongoing biting effectively, you will most likely need to implement program changes as well as specific techniques to help the child who is biting. What follows here are strategies and techniques tailored to some of the specific reasons children bite.

Strategies and Techniques Related to Development

Chapter 1 identified developmental issues that can provide context for biting. They include teething, oral-motor development, sensory exploration, learning about cause and effect, imitation, spatial awareness, emerging autonomy, expressive language development, a need for attention, and holding on and letting go. Here are some strategies and techniques for dealing with each.

TEETHING

▸ Check with parents to see what they are doing for their child's teething pain. If they are using something to soothe gums, ask them to bring a supply (with instructions) to use in the program. Be sure to consult your state's licensing regulations and your program's policy on the use of over-the-counter medications with children, especially medications that go in children's mouths.

▸ Make sure you have a variety of objects that children can chew on to relieve the pain and pressure of teething. These might include teething toys, frozen foods that are chewy and won't cause choking, and clean cloths that have been frozen.

▸ Actively encourage toddlers who are teething to bite on these items; you are telling children what you *do* want them to bite rather than simply telling them that you *don't* want them to bite other children after they've already done so.

ORAL-MOTOR DEVELOPMENT

▸ Provide many toys and materials that work by having children blow. These include bubble wands, rings, and pipes that children can use to blow bubbles;

musical instruments that children blow into to produce sound; toys with tubes that children blow into to make small objects rise; and party favors that unroll when children blow into them. Have children blow through straws to paint, to make small toy cars move, and so forth.

▶ Provide materials specifically for children to gnaw on. Some children may benefit from chewing on special toothbrushes, such as Nuk brushes, which have soft bristles on one end and a hard nub on the other. These are different from teething rings because children can use their molars. Special care must be taken to ensure that children gnaw on only their own toothbrush and that gnawing toys are kept clean and sanitized.

▶ Provide foods with a variety of textures. Children need soft food such as cooked vegetables and bread to munch, hard foods such as toast and raw vegetable slices to crunch, and chewy foods such as fruits and diced meats to chew. Allow children enough time to munch, crunch, and chew their food.

SENSORY EXPLORATION

▶ Since toddlers often explore with their mouths, make sure you have a plentiful and varied supply of toys they *can* put in their mouths. Have a plan for cleaning such toys. One recommendation is to pick up any toy you have seen a child mouth and set it aside to be cleaned (that's why you need so many of them). The toys are then washed with soap and water, sprayed with a bleach and water solution (one part bleach to ten parts water), and left to air-dry.

▶ Provide many opportunities and materials for sensory play. Offer supervised sand and water play. Have sensory art materials, such as fingerpaints and playdough, available for supervised exploration.

▶ Give children opportunities to explore a variety of textures, spaces, and places. Provide tunnels, small forts, and different kinds of surfaces for children to crawl on.

LEARNING ABOUT CAUSE AND EFFECT

▶ Provide toddlers with plenty of cause-and-effect toys. These include toys and activity books in which they can make something happen by pushing a button, turning a knob, lifting a flap, pulling a tab, and so on.

▶ Offer art materials so toddlers can make colors and designs appear by wielding a brush or marker.

▶ Help toddlers understand "What happens when . . ." and "What happens if . . ." by describing the cause-and-effect relationships you see a child engaging in. Use phrases such as these:

- "Look at that. When you moved the paintbrush across the paper, you made all that blue."
- "Every time you pull the string, that little door opens, and you can see the clown."

▶ When a child bites, use cause-and-effect statements to describe the painful result of the biting, such as "When you bit Maura, it hurt her, and she cried." Make sure that the child does not profit from biting. Do not allow the child to keep a toy that was obtained by biting the child who originally had it. This way the child learns, "If you bite someone to get a toy, you can't keep the toy."

▶ Help toddlers recognize the cause and effect of positive behavior. "When you got more playdough, Isabel could use it, too, and she likes that." "When you helped pick up the toys, we got to go outside to play sooner."

IMITATION

▶ When you suspect a toddler might be biting because he is imitating another child, provide lots of examples of other, more acceptable behavior for the child to imitate. Model nurturing, sharing, respectful, polite, empathetic behavior. Show positive ways to handle anger and frustration. When you say, "I was so frustrated when I couldn't get the jar open," or when you respond to a child who is angry with "You are so angry with Tenzin because he took the truck you had," you are giving the child a new behavior to imitate.

▶ Stop any play biting that you may be doing with toddlers. Ask other adults to do the same. (See pages 11–12 for more information on play biting.)

SPATIAL AWARENESS

▶ Recognize that toddlers like to experiment with space, and provide them with many small areas that are just the right size. Allow toddlers to take toys off low, sturdy shelves so they can sit on those shelves themselves.

▶ Create simple and safe obstacle courses so toddlers can experiment with going through cardboard box tunnels, over low pillows, and around stationary objects. These obstacle courses can be created, rearranged, and dismantled as needed.

▶ Help toddlers become aware of how close they are to other children. When they are too close to another child or, in some cases, almost on top of another child, use words and redirection to help them move and give the other child some space. "You are too close to Darnell. He can't move around. Come and sit here." (Indicate where the child should sit.)

▶ If two children are often too close to each other, try sitting on the floor with them with your legs out in front of you. Have one child on one side of you and the other child on the other side. The children are near each other, but you are helping organize the space by the placement of your legs.

▶ If a child is really struggling with space issues, have him sit at the end of a table rather than in the middle with other children on each side. Another strategy is to let him use a toy that defines his space for him, such as a toy car he can sit in. Of course, you'll have to have other toy cars for some of the other children.

EMERGING AUTONOMY

▶ Toddlers need many opportunities to feel powerful and competent while still feeling and being safe. You can help foster the child's sense of having power by structuring choices—letting the child make a choice and then respecting that choice.

▶ Toddlers do best with a simple choice between two alternatives, both of which are acceptable. For example, you can offer the toddler the choice between fingerpainting or using brushes to paint, or between putting the napkin on the table first or the cup on the table first.

▶ When the toddler makes the choice, reinforce the power of choosing and support the choice by commenting, "You decided to put the napkin on first." Then make sure you let the child follow through.

▶ Try to provide as many opportunities for choosing as possible, because so often you must place limits on toddlers' behavior to keep them safe.

EXPRESSIVE LANGUAGE DEVELOPMENT

▶ Always respond to children's verbal communications, including babbling, jabbering, words, and phrases. This lets them understand that verbal communication is valuable.

▶ Name objects, materials, and people. Children's brains love to make connections, and when two things happen at the same time, a connection is made. So when you hand a child a spoon and say, "Here's your spoon," the child makes the connection between the object and its name. This helps children develop vocabulary to describe what they want, which can reduce their frustration at not being able to express themselves. It also gives them a way of communicating other than biting.

▶ Put words with actions. Describe what you are doing and what the children are doing. "You put the car on top of the table. You're using your hand to make it go fast."

▶ Have conversations with children. Listen to what they are saying. Follow their lead, add some more information, or ask a question, then wait for the child to continue the conversation. These conversations help extend children's language. Children are more likely to participate in such conversations and speak more than when adults initiate or dominate conversations.

A NEED FOR ATTENTION

If you think a child is biting to get attention, try giving him lots of attention before he resorts to biting. Give attention freely and lavishly; don't make the child wait for, ask for, or earn it. Often the child who needs positive attention the most is the one we are least likely to give it to. Make an effort to notice and comment on all the child's acceptable behaviors—being curious, helping, creating, and so forth. In this way, you can teach the child who had been biting that other, more positive behaviors are even more likely to get your attention.

You can also use specific preemptive interactions to give children more attention. *Preempt* means to take action in order to prevent an anticipated event from happening. In the instance of toddlers and attention, the anticipated event is acting out to get attention, and the key words here are "to take action." We are literally taking action to give toddlers attention without waiting for them to seek it out. The power of this approach is that toddlers experience getting positive attention on an ongoing and reliable basis from us. They don't have to wonder if they'll get attention; they experience that they will. And the more they know they will get attention, the less they have to initiate their own actions to get it.

Here are several preemptive interactions that help you give toddlers attention:

▶ When toddlers come into the room, greet them by name and add a warm, positive statement about their presence. "Kylie, you're here! I've been waiting for you." "Ryan, here you are. Ta-da!" This lets the child know both that you noticed (paid attention to) his or her arrival and that he or she is important to you.

▶ Throughout the day, look for informal opportunities to catch the eye of a child. When that happens, maintain eye contact and send the child a positive message, such as a wave, a thumbs-up, a wink, or a blown kiss. Again, this sends the message that you noticed the child and that you like him or her.

▶ Use preemptive attention comments. These are positive comments that call attention to what the child is currently doing. As such, you can use them throughout the day. Start by noticing something a child is doing. You don't have to wait for some kind of amazing accomplishment; you can comment on anything the child is doing. Speak warmly and personally to the child using a preemptive attention comment that follows this model:

- "I see you making that truck go up the ramp. I see you."

- "I hear you saying the names of all those pictures. I hear you."

- This model begins and ends with the words "I see you" or "I hear you." This sends children a clear message that you are paying attention to what they are doing because you tell them you are. You strengthen this by describing what they are actually doing, so you prove you are paying attention to them.

▶ Use these interactions freely and lavishly when you sense that a child needs more attention. They are valuable interactions for all children at any time. You don't have to wait until someone is biting. This is the very definition of *preemptive*.

HOLDING ON AND LETTING GO

▶ Give the toddler lots of opportunities to practice physical holding on and letting go. This can be in the form of two favorite toddler activities, "pick up little things and put them into containers" and "pick up, carry around, and dump." Both give the child the opportunity to practice and enjoy holding on and letting go.

▶ Work on emotional letting go as well. Help toddlers who are having a difficult time with separations by telling them, for example, "You're so sad when your daddy has to go. It's hard for you when Daddy leaves. He will go to work, and then he will come back after we play outside."

▶ Children who are having trouble holding on and letting go may not be able to control and "let go" of urine or feces, so hold off on toilet learning.

Strategies and Techniques Related to Expressing Feelings

Chapter 1 listed the common feelings that get expressed through biting, including frustration and anger, tension, anxiety, and excitement. Here are some strategies and techniques for dealing with each.

FRUSTRATION AND ANGER

▸ Capitalize on toddlers' desire to imitate by expressing your own frustration and anger in words. Teach the child to say an emphatic "No!" or "Stop it!" to another child who is trying to take a toy or book away from him. Encourage children to say, "I don't like it when . . ." or "I am so mad when . . ." Being able to express feelings with heartfelt words may prevent children from expressing those feelings with their teeth.

▸ Learn to recognize signs of frustration in the child. When you see him begin to get frustrated, use redirection to help him out of the situation. For example, a six-piece puzzle may be too difficult for him. Be prepared to redirect him to a puzzle with three pieces so he can experience success instead of frustration.

TENSION

▸ Observe the child so you will recognize signs of mounting tension.

▸ Help relieve tension in the child's mouth and jaw by gently massaging the joint where the jaw meets the skull (just in front of the ear) with circular motions. But don't just swoop down and begin manipulating the face of a child who is already tense. To be more respectful and effective, approach the child from the front and make eye contact. Begin by gently tracing circles on the back of her hand while using a soft, rhythmic voice to say, "I'm making little circles on your hand." Then gradually move up to the arm while saying, "I'm making little circles on your arm." Work up to the child's shoulders. "I'm making little circles on your shoulder." Finally, move your fingers to the spot you want to massage in front of the ear. "I'm making little circles by your ear." Massage is so calming that you may want to do it regularly to get the children in your program used to it. Then when you need to use it to relieve the tension that may be a factor in biting, children will be more likely to accept it.

▸ Step in to redirect when a child is getting into a potentially tense situation. For example, a child may try to get into a private space that another child is already occupying. If you can help him find another space or another way of meeting his need for privacy, he is less likely to bite.

▶ Provide more gross-motor activities—such as moving the arms, legs, and torso to music—to relieve tension.

▶ Try going outside more often to relieve the tension associated with being in confined spaces.

ANXIETY

▶ Use your own observations and information from the child's parents to understand why the child may be anxious or what she may be worried about. Use reassuring language with the child. "I'm going to be right here when you need me."

▶ Provide a calm atmosphere by playing soothing music and giving the child one-on-one attention during the day.

▶ Make sure there is a place for the child to go to get away from the pressures of the group. This might be a quiet corner with soft pillows or a "house" made out of a big cardboard box and just big enough for one.

▶ Help the child calm herself by allowing her to suck a pacifier or her thumb (if she already does this) or by using a comfort object, such as a favorite blanket from home.

▶ Give the child plenty of time to eat, make transitions, use the toilet, and so on to reduce feelings of pressure.

▶ Soothe the child at naptime with back rubs and songs.

EXCITEMENT

▶ Encourage toddlers to develop a variety of physical (nonbiting) expressions of excitement. For example, have them clap happily, jump up and down, dance around, and yell, "Yay!" Do this with them when the occasion calls for excitement.

▶ Be aware that some children have intense reactions to almost everything. This is part of their inborn temperament, and you will notice that these children seem to react more quickly and with more vigor than other children. When they are excited, this inborn tendency to react intensely may result in biting. During moments of great excitement, you may want to position yourself near them to direct their excitement to an appropriate action.

Shadowing: A Last-Ditch Technique

When you have exhausted all other possibilities, you may want to try having someone shadow the child who is biting. Shadowing involves having one staff person stay with the child, positioning herself where she can always intercept a bite. Because one staff person must be devoted to watching and staying with just one child, shadowing is often difficult for programs to do. Shadowing requires intense vigilance, but it often works. The staff person shadowing the child is usually able to redirect the child before biting occurs, showing the child different, more acceptable behavior. This means that instead of biting, the child is going through the day *not* biting, and this can become his new behavior.

Parents often ask that programs shadow children who are biting as one of the first techniques to try because it seems like the most logical intervention. However, a carefully crafted, appropriate plan will ultimately work better because it will address the reasons for the biting. This is especially true if there are factors in the child care environment that are contributing to biting. Shadowing might stop a child from biting in the moment, but if the difficult environmental factors are still in place, the child is almost sure to bite again after the shadowing stops. You should try a complete plan of other strategies for several weeks, adjusting as needed, before resorting to shadowing. Remember that you are looking for improvement, not perfection. If the biting diminishes, stick with your plan. Changes are stressful for children, and giving up on your plan when it is working can bring biting back.

A less intensive version of shadowing can be used successfully when one child repeatedly bites the same child. Try bringing the two children together for very closely supervised play—perhaps sensory play at a sand or water table. Have an adult place herself between the children and supervise, interacting with both children and standing ready to make an intervention if the situation warrants it. This gives both children the opportunity to experience bite-free interaction. Further, it allows the child who has been biting to get positive attention for positive interactions.

"But Is This Fair to the Other Children?"

When programs need to work more intensively with children who are biting, the fairness question is often raised. "Is it fair to give this one child so much attention? What about the other kids?" This issue was raised by directors in our focus group, and it is worth considering and thinking through. There are two important concepts that relate to this issue. First, in the United States, fairness is seen as a virtue, and many Americans are quite vigilant and often quite vocal about it. The very symbol of our justice system, the blindfolded statue holding the scales of justice, signals fairness—the same treatment for everyone. Even though we recognize that this is not always the case, and even though we have an oft-used saying, "Life isn't fair," we wish it would be. We often see fairness as an ideal, and we notice when things do not appear fair to us. Second, we almost always think of fairness in terms of equal amounts, portions, size, and so on. If we put these two concepts together, we can see how the idea that giving extra time and attention to one child in a group raises the fairness question. All children are not getting exactly the same amount of time and attention, so it looks unfair to us. We want things to be fair, and this is not fair.

The amount and kind of attention we give to children who need help to stop biting is not about failing to be fair; it is about meeting needs. Let's go back and think a little more carefully about the concept that *fair* means *the same amount*. Suppose we embraced that concept and decided to be scrupulously fair to the toddlers in our classroom. We looked at our daily schedule and figured out that we could give each toddler seven uninterrupted minutes of time on our lap each day for individual attention. That would be absolutely, unequivocally fair because it's the same amount of time for everyone. However, not all toddlers want and need the same amount of time on your lap. Those who work with toddlers have almost surely seen children who love to be on their caregiver's lap. If they could, they would have themselves surgically implanted on their favorite caregiver's lap. Then there are other children who like their caregivers very much but don't really want to spend much time on their laps. These children might love a good hug or a quick book on the teacher's lap, but then they want to get off and move on. So, what seemed like a very fair seven minutes is not nearly enough for one child and is way, way too much for another. In the quest to be scrupulously fair, we would not have met the needs of either child.

Many of the suggestions in this chapter do not involve a great deal of time or take attention away from others. They might be a matter of changes to the environment, new or different activities, improved interactions with children, and support through physical proximity. Our focus may be on the child who is biting, but that doesn't mean all our time is going to that child. And, of course, as the biting gradually stops, that's good for all the children.

We are often amazed at how perceptive even very young children are, and how easily they notice when someone is upset and needs help. We see toddlers offer their own blankies to other toddlers who are crying. We see them gently pat someone who looks sad. We hear them ask, "Okay? Okay?" when another child appears to be upset. It is reassuring to toddlers when they see their caregivers giving attention to children who need it. Of course, we need to be mindful that other children may want more attention at these times. If the other children feel they are not getting enough attention, they will find ways to let you know. You can find a number of suggestions for giving children individual attention in group settings on pages 40–41.

When you have decided which program changes and specific strategies and techniques best fit the ongoing biting in your classroom, you are ready to put your plan in place and begin to implement it.

Implement the Plan

Decide on a length of time to try the plan, allow enough time to implement the changes, and follow them consistently. Usually at least a week or two is needed before you can expect to see significant changes in the children. Share your written plan with the parents of all the children in the program. (See page 108 for a sample letter that illustrates how to do this effectively.)

Then begin the trial period. The plan will need to be followed consistently in order to work. If you plan to offer the water table every day, but you only manage to get it open once or twice during the week, you probably haven't made a big enough change to affect the biting. This doesn't mean that the change didn't work—you haven't really made the change yet. Ask your administrator for support and encouragement during this time. And don't forget to keep observing carefully. You may discover new information about the child who is biting, the children who are being bitten, or the program. New information can help you revise or fine-tune your plan so it keeps working.

Finally, evaluate your progress. At the end of the specified trial period, determine whether the biting has decreased. If it has, celebrate your success and keep going. Don't measure your success by whether the biting has stopped completely; that's probably not a realistic short-term goal. If the number of attempted and actual bites has decreased, the plan is working. The biting will continue to decrease over time if you keep observing children and meeting their needs, and eventually it will stop completely.

If the biting hasn't decreased at all, you will need to modify your plan or create a new one. To do that, you will have to review your observations during the trial period and think about what seemed to work and why as well as what didn't work and why. You will have to think about what parts of the plan you were able to implement and what you didn't do quite the way you thought you would. Then modify your plan, taking these insights into account. It's a good idea not to change your strategies completely from one week to the next; rather, keep your plan pretty much the same and fine-tune it to make it work better for you and for the children.

Share Your Plan with Parents

Parents need to know what you are doing about ongoing biting. Sharing your plan openly in a letter demonstrates to parents your willingness to admit that a problem exists and shows them you know what you are going to do to address ongoing biting. This encourages them to have confidence in the program.

Appendix A contains a sample letter to parents explaining your plan to address ongoing biting. This sample deals with a hypothetical biting situation. It is designed to help you formulate your own letter based on your plan for dealing with ongoing biting in your program.

When the Plan Doesn't Go according to Plan

Even the most carefully and thoughtfully developed plans may need adjustments. While everyone involved wants this to work, most people also want it to work quickly. Some people may even be hoping for an overnight success story. You may well see some positive results quite quickly if your plan includes changes to the environment and you make those changes. If the plan includes helping children learn new behaviors, it is much more likely to take some time. Children need both time to learn new skills and many, many opportunities to practice them. When and if a situation does not improve as quickly as expected (or wanted), it is easy to become discouraged. Be patient, purposeful, and consistent in carrying out your plan. Be honest with yourselves and honest with parents if you need to adjust your plan. Finally, acknowledge, appreciate, and share the progress you have made. Remember and believe that all progress counts.

Helping the Child Who Is Being Bitten Repeatedly

With so much attention focused on the child who is biting, it is easy to forget that the child who is being bitten may also need help. Anytime a child is bitten, we need to provide first aid, comfort, support, and reassurance. But when we notice a particular child is being bitten again and again, that child may need more help from us. We don't want children to feel helpless, and we don't want children to become comfortable in the role of victim. Learning to stand up for themselves is an important social and emotional goal for young children. We also want to help the child who is repeatedly being bitten, because that child may respond by biting in return.

First, let the child know that it is all right to be mad (or frightened or worried) when someone bites him. You may have to tell him, "You don't like it when Mary bites you. She hurt you."

Second, help children learn to say no when another child is hurting them. This language may range from a simple, emphatic "No!" or "Stop!" to longer phrases, such as "Don't bite me." Model the words and tone for children to use. It will be much easier for them to learn to stand up for themselves if they can start by imitating your words and tone instead of trying to come up with their own. This also gives you another possibility for preventing a bite: when you hear children using their new words, respond quickly, and you may be able to help them solve a problem before one of them gets bitten. Specific suggestions for helping children learn to stand up for themselves are covered in "Helping the Child Who Was Bitten" on pages 20–21.

As with any technique or strategy, you need to base your actions on observations. If you are observing a child who is being bitten a great deal, you may discover that something the child is doing is resulting in her being bitten. An example might be a girl grabbing a toy right out of the hands of a boy, who then bites her. You don't want the boy to bite, and you don't want the girl to be bitten. At the same time, you don't want the girl to take the toy away from the boy. In this case, you need to redirect the girl toward a different toy and help her begin to understand that she may not grab a toy away from someone else. Both children need to learn different behavior.

This is also an opportunity to give the child who is being bitten some advice. This advice falls into the category of cause and effect.

When you grab his toys away from him, he bites you. When you want a toy that someone else has, let me help you ask for it.

When you get so close to Mariah, she bites you. Mariah doesn't want anyone to get so close to her. You can get really close to me. Then we can go to Mariah together.

For in-depth examples of observation techniques and planning, see appendix B.

CHAPTER 4

Working with Parents
and Other Community Members

Biting in child care programs can strain even the best relationships between parents and programs. Child Care Solutions has found that parents want two things when it comes to biting:

▶ They want programs and providers to take it as seriously as they do.

▶ They want the biting to stop.

Caregivers and Parents Have Different Perspectives

Caregivers and directors in child care programs serving toddlers often claim that "parents just don't understand about biting." In one sense, this is true. They don't understand biting the same way caregivers understand it, and that's not surprising. Experienced caregivers and directors most likely have dealt with many biting incidents in the course of their work with toddlers. They have probably read books and articles and attended training related to biting. The sheer amount of biting they deal with shapes their understanding of biting. On the other hand, parents may have very little experience with biting because they do not interact with the number of toddlers that caregivers do year after year. It is almost guaranteed that parents will look at biting differently than caregivers do. The chart below presents some of these differences very clearly:

When it comes to biting, caregivers	When it comes to biting, parents
are not surprised when toddlers bite;	are very surprised when toddlers bite—sometimes even shocked;
know that biting is not unusual behavior for toddlers and doesn't necessarily indicate something is seriously wrong;	assume something must be terribly wrong either with the child or with the program when toddlers bite;
know toddlers bite for many reasons;	may see toddler biting as a deliberate act of aggression;
know it may take some time before the biting stops;	believe that biting can be stopped quickly and easily;
know they can't guarantee there will be no biting.	believe biting can be "guaranteed against."

I developed this chart after conversations with many parents and caregivers during conflicts over toddler biting. In talking with parents, I began to identify some common themes in their responses to biting and in their comments and questions about the child care programs. I listed these themes and shared them with toddler caregivers in workshops. In workshop after workshop, caregivers recognized the themes and had experienced parents' responses reflecting those themes. These responses do not necessarily apply to every parent, but in conflicts about biting, they are often present.

It is essential that caregivers and directors understand their difference in perspective; it is equally important that they *acknowledge* parents' perspective on biting. They do not have to agree with it, but they must accept that this is the way parents look at biting. Since our actions are based on our particular perspective, when we understand parents' beliefs about biting, we are better able to understand the depth of their feelings and the certainty of their convictions about biting. We can also understand their reactions, suggestions, and demands. Then we can use these insights to determine what we must do to be effective with parents when toddlers are biting.

While we must acknowledge the parents' perspective, we cannot base our approach to biting on it. Our approach to biting must be based on our knowledge of why children bite and of developmentally appropriate practices to help reduce the biting. Nevertheless, we can use our knowledge and understanding of the parents' perspective to create effective approaches to *parents*.

PARENTS' COMMON REACTIONS

The following are three common reactions of parents to providers and to biting situations in their children's child care programs.

Parents often say their concerns are being taken lightly. We have found that parents are upset when programs calmly explain biting in terms of "normal toddler development." For parents, saying that something is "normal" implies that it is to be expected and tolerated. This is upsetting for parents because biting is not something *they* expected, and they most certainly do not want to tolerate anything that hurts their children.

Parents often feel that the teachers and the director don't care that their children were bitten. Teachers who have cared for toddlers for many years have probably dealt with hundreds of biting incidents. Over the years they have likely developed effective techniques to address biting and may also have worked hard to put everything they have learned about biting into explanations and information for parents. Sometimes the very words they have carefully chosen to inform and reassure parents may be interpreted by parents as not taking the biting seriously. When caregivers talk with parents about biting, they must make sure to express genuine regret about it and recognize and acknowledge parents' shock, pain, and (if it is present) outrage.

Parents often report that when biting becomes an ongoing problem, teachers and directors tell them they're taking care of it but offer no specific information on how. When parents don't see any changes in either the program or the amount of biting, they suspect nothing is being done. Then they feel the program is either unable or unwilling to address the biting. When parents lose confidence in the program, they may resort to threats of taking their children out of it or demands that children who bite be expelled. When parents know that specific steps are being taken to address the biting, they are much more likely to be supportive.

What Can Parents Reasonably Expect of Programs?

Here is a list of what parents can reasonably expect from their child's program when it comes to biting. Use it as a quick checklist to assess if you are doing everything you can to support and reassure parents when biting is an issue in your program.

Parents can reasonably expect that a good child care program will

▶ put children's safety first and provide appropriate first aid as well as comfort, support, and advice to any child who is bitten;

- ▶ provide appropriate programming for their toddlers, thus reducing the likelihood of biting;

- ▶ help children who are biting for any reason to learn not to bite;

- ▶ give parents current information or resources on biting;

- ▶ ensure that teachers have adequate knowledge and training to deal appropriately and effectively with biting;

- ▶ take parents' concerns seriously and treat parents with understanding and respect;

- ▶ tell parents what specific steps are being taken to address biting and explain the reasons for those steps;

- ▶ respond to their questions, concerns, and suggestions—even when the response to their suggestions is "no";

- ▶ be willing to schedule parent-teacher conferences about biting at a time when parents can come;

- ▶ keep their child's identity confidential if he or she bites to avoid labeling or confrontations with other families that will slow the process of learning not to bite.

Appendix A contains a version of this list incorporated into a letter to parents. You can use a letter like this to let parents know what they can expect from your program, and parents can use it as a checklist to evaluate the way your program handles an actual biting episode. You can ask parents to check whether or not you did the things you said you would do. This may help focus parents' attention on program responses that are appropriate rather than on inappropriate responses they may suggest.

Note that the last item in the letter refers to keeping *their* child's identity confidential if she or he bites. We have used this wording to help parents identify with the child who is biting. Some parents feel that the staff is withholding information from them when they keep a child's name confidential. It's important to help parents understand why confidentiality is necessary to stop the biting and why confidentiality is a positive thing. You can also use the phrasing in the list above in your letter to parents.

Saying No: When You Can't Give Parents What They Want

Sometimes parents ask for something we cannot or are not willing to give them. Parents often call Child Care Solutions to say that all they want is a guarantee that their child will not be bitten, and they truly believe that good programs should be able to give them that. After all, "I pay good money for that child care; they should at least be able to make sure no one bites my child."

While we acknowledge that such a guarantee would be wonderful, we can't give it because we truthfully can't make that promise to parents. Child Care Solutions gently tells parents that any program offering such a guarantee is lying to them, fooling itself, or willing to do things to children that they don't even want to imagine.

Parents may ask programs to

- ▶ keep "the biter" away from their child;

- ▶ give them the name of the child who is biting their son or daughter;

- ▶ kick out the child who is biting;

- ▶ punish the biting child by withholding snacks or activities;

- ▶ demand that "the biter" be tested for HIV/AIDS and/or hepatitis;

- ▶ allow them to handle the biting situation themselves by punishing the other child's parents;

- ▶ allow them to discipline the child who bit their son or daughter;

- ▶ suspend the child who bit for a few weeks to "break the biting cycle."

Sometimes these suggestions and demands catch us off guard because, at least to us, they are so obviously the wrong thing to do. But we must take into consideration the emotional nature of parents' responses to biting. In the heat of the moment, parents may want to punish the child who bit or the child's parents. Sometimes their demands are an attempt to impress on us just how serious this biting is. This is especially the case when parents demand that the child who bit be tested for HIV/AIDS. Parents may also want to force something on the child or her parents just as the bite was forced on their child.

Parents want decisive action, and they are more than willing to give us suggestions. Teachers need to be responsive and respectful even when they say no to inappropriate suggestions. This is not easy, but it is a child care provider's responsibility. Here are some examples of responses that respect and recognize the perspective of the parent but still do not comply with their suggestion or demand.

You would like to have a child who is biting stay home for a few weeks so he can have some "bite-free" time and maybe break the biting cycle. And the child may indeed not bite during the weeks he would be out of the program. But when he came back, if nothing had changed here or if he hadn't learned different behavior, he would just start biting again. I want us to spend our energy and time improving our program and helping him learn different behavior.

Seeing that bite on your child must be so frightening. It looks so awful. Now you're worried about AIDS because of the saliva and broken skin. We worried about biting and AIDS, too, so we checked to see whether AIDS is spread by biting. We found out that it isn't. I can give you a copy of that information. This may take care of that worry, but biting is still very upsetting. See pages 78–79 for information on HIV/AIDS.

You're so angry that your child was bitten, and you want me to let you punish the child who bit her. But this is something I am not willing to do. It might make you feel better, but it would not help the child learn different behavior. This is not easy for me to say, because I like to be able to give parents what they want. I would like to tell you what we have decided to do about the biting. (This is a good lead-in to sharing the plan you have developed.)

Parents may also try to put pressure on caregivers to break confidentiality and tell them the name of the child who is biting. They may say they have other ways of finding out, so the caregiver might as well tell them. It is quite likely they may find out who bit their child because their child may be able to tell them. It is difficult to respond when a parent says, "You might as well tell me, because I'm going to find out anyway." Here is a response that recognizes the parent may indeed learn the name of the child who bit from someone else and that helps the caregiver maintain professionalism:

"You might hear who bit your child from someone else, but you will not hear it from me. I work hard to maintain confidentiality. I would not give out the name of your child, and I won't give out the name of another child. You can count on me to work very hard at solving the biting situation, and you can count on me to keep confidentiality."

Responding When Parents Demand That a Biting Child Be Expelled

One of the most difficult dilemmas related to biting occurs when a parent or parents demand that the child who is biting be expelled from the program. This message is usually delivered as an ultimatum: "Either you get rid of the biter, or I am taking my child out of the program." Experienced directors will almost certainly recognize this situation and know the anguish it produces. They are caught in the customer service dilemma that results when doing what is right for children may not be popular with parents who are the customers. Directors want to work with staff to help children who are biting, but they worry about the financial impact of losing other children.

In my years consulting with early childhood programs on biting, I have learned some important lessons about this issue. First, when a program had made the decision to work on the biting and was faithfully implementing the plan we had developed together, the director did not agree to expel the biting child. Second, only a very few parents actually removed their children. Third, and most important, I learned that parents do not take their children out of a program because of biting if they like the program, if they've had good experiences with it, and if they know what you are doing to address the biting and can see that you are working on it.

This is encouraging. It indicates what we can do to keep parents from feeling that expelling a biting child is the only solution to the situation. We must offer a high-quality program that is warm and responsive to children. We must be open with parents and work as genuine partners with them. Taken together, these will almost surely result in parents having good experiences with our program and liking it. The information and examples in this book are a blueprint for responding effectively to biting and communicating clearly with parents. When we put this information and these examples to work, *we* will know what we're doing about the biting. And when we communicate it clearly to parents, *they* will know what we're doing about the biting. Finally, as we carry out our plans, parents can see that we are working on the situation because we will be doing what we said we were going to do. All of this works together to build a sense of parent confidence in our program.

Responding to Well-Intentioned Bad Advice

Over the years, members of the Task Force on Biting have received a great deal of advice from parents and others on how to handle biting. Some of these suggestions have been sound, but many have been ineffective, some impossible, and a few actually cruel. If you care for toddlers, you have probably encountered (or will encounter) these or similar suggestions when biting incidents occur:

- ▶ forcing something into the child's mouth (people have suggested vinegar, lemon juice, pepper, soap, even cigarette butts)
- ▶ punishing the child at home that evening
- ▶ bribing the child not to bite
- ▶ biting the child back

▸ having the other child bite back

▸ spanking the child

▸ making the child go to the director's office

▸ popping the child under the chin after biting

▸ keeping the child away from other children or away from one child
in particular

Occasionally the suggestions are offered out of a desperate desire to do *something*. More often the advice is well-intentioned, and people offer it because they think it will work. They may even share an anecdote to prove their point. More than once a parent has said, "Well, my child bit one time. I bit her back, and let me tell you, she never bit again!" This may be true, but it doesn't necessarily mean that the child stopped biting because the parent bit her back. It also does not mean that biting children back will stop them from biting in other situations. We have heard from parents who bit their children back and ended up with furious toddlers on a biting rampage.

To respond effectively to parents who make these suggestions, you need to know why these are inappropriate responses to biting. Acknowledging the perspective of the person offering the advice is the first step to an effective response. Being able to begin your response in a sincere tone with something such as, "I know it sounds like that might stop the biting . . . ," makes it much more likely that the rest of your response will be taken seriously. Let's take a look at these suggestions one by one to see why they don't work and why no good program would ever use them.

Forcing something into the child's mouth. This may be suggested as an effective punishment. The reasoning behind the technique is that toddlers will stop biting to stop the unpleasant tastes being forced into their mouths or will associate biting with the unpleasant experience and therefore stop. Good programs and providers, however, do not guide or correct children's behavior in ways that hurt or frighten the child. Toddlers who have things forced into their mouths will most likely be confused, scared, or furious. They will also become distrustful of the adults who did it. This is a prescription to encourage biting, not stop it.

Punishing the child at home. Most parents feel they should do something to address the biting. They don't want their children to bite, and they feel they need to have some kind of response. Since they weren't at the scene of the biting when it occurred, they try to punish the child later at home. This may make the parent feel better, but it's ineffective because the child won't connect the punishment to the biting.

Bribing the child not to bite. As with punishment, parents usually try bribery because they want to do *something* to stop the biting. And it's important for teachers to understand that parents may really believe it will work. Since adults are able to understand the concept of being rewarded for something they do (or don't do), it is tempting to think that toddlers understand this as well. But toddlers don't make the connection between the action and the promised reward and don't make decisions about behavior based on delayed rewards. If a toddler does remember anything about the statement, "If you don't bite, I'll give you a sticker [or some other special treat]," it is likely to be the reward. Toddlers have been known to run to their parents at the end of a day punctuated by biting to excitedly await the promised reward. When parents find out that the child has bitten several times that day, they express surprise that their child still expects the reward.

Biting the child back. This seems to be the prevailing advice given by parents as a surefire way to get toddlers to stop biting. The reasoning is that if toddlers experience the pain of biting, they'll stop biting others. This technique is usually ineffective because what toddlers actually experience is an adult biting them for no reason that the toddler can figure out. Furthermore, biting back is ineffective because children learn behavior that adults model for them. If adults bite, children will learn to bite from them. If adults bite children, children learn it's okay to bite if you're bigger, stronger, or in the right. This will not stop them from biting.

Finally, the most damaging aspect of biting back is the effect it has on children's trust and sense of security with staff in a child care program. Children need to know that they can trust their caregivers and that they are safe at child care and at home, which is not true if caregivers bite them. Children who don't feel secure are more likely to bite.

Having the other child bite back. This is a variation on having the adult bite the child back and is ineffective for the same reasons. In this case, you are actually teaching children to bite by allowing (or perhaps even insisting) that a child bite! This technique is cruel to both children.

Spanking the child. This is yet another technique involving physical punishment to address biting. It is ineffective and damaging for the same reasons cited in the section on biting the child back. In addition, most states do not permit corporal punishment in child care centers.

Making the child go to the director's office. This technique has actually been written into the plan of some child care programs, often to show the parents that something is being done about the biting. While it does remove the child from the room, it does nothing to address the reason the child is biting or to guide the child in learning other behavior. When the child returns to the room, nothing has changed, including the biting.

Popping the child under the chin after biting. Apparently this is sometimes used to train puppies not to bite. It may be suggested on the basis of "If it works with puppies, it should work with kids." Children, however, need to learn how not to bite, and this technique doesn't help them. In addition, it is likely to frighten, startle, or hurt the child and damage his sense of trust and security in the child care program. These results are likely to cause more biting. Can anyone imagine caregivers hitting toddlers on the nose with a rolled-up newspaper every time they have an accident while they are learning to use the toilet?

Keeping the child away from other children or from one child in particular. This is a seemingly commonsense approach to keeping a particular child safe. The problem is that it is almost impossible to limit toddlers to certain areas of the room or to make particular children off-limits. In addition, there may be several biting patterns going on, and caregivers could not possibly keep straight who was not supposed to play with whom.

From a philosophical viewpoint, keeping children apart so they can't interact is the complete opposite of what we are trying to facilitate. If we want children to learn to interact without biting, they need the opportunity to play together. When biting occurs, the task of teaching children how to be with one another becomes more difficult, which highlights the need to do it well. When there seems to be a recurring pattern of one child choosing a particular child to bite, caregivers need to increase their supervision of those particular children, but caregivers can't be expected to keep the children apart.

When responding to inappropriate suggestions, some toddler caregivers like to use a standard phrase, such as "Oh, we're not allowed to do that in our program" or "It's against state regulations." This sounds as though they agree that the suggestion is a good one and would try it if it weren't for the rules and regulations. It's tempting to say something like this because it puts you on the parents' side for the moment. It looks as though you agree, and you are united with parents against the program or the state. This approach may seem easier than giving parents the bad news that you don't agree with them and possibly getting into an argument.

Unfortunately, siding with parents in this manner usually backfires, because it's not really honest. If you helped create the program's plan to address the biting and you understand why a parent's suggestion would not work, giving parents the impression that you agree with them is not telling the truth. It gives parents the idea that even the staff disagree on what to do about the biting. This is confusing for parents, who then don't know whom to believe or what is right for their children. Dishonesty can also make parents feel as though staff are not willing to take responsibility for the program's decisions. This can weaken parents' confidence in the program, making it harder for them to trust that staff are really doing the best they can to stop the biting. In the end, your job becomes harder because parents who don't feel they can trust the program will give you much less support when you need it.

If you don't feel that you can explain the reasons adequately, or if you are afraid of a confrontation, it's okay to suggest that a parent talk with the director. You can say something such as, "I know it sounds like that would work, but it really doesn't. This is hard for me to explain, and Jennifer can talk about it much more clearly than I can." Let Jennifer know you have referred the parents to her, and then work on developing explanations in your own words so you will be able to share them directly with parents in the future.

Sometimes it's true that caregivers don't agree with the plan that has been made and would like to use one of the methods outlined earlier to address the biting. If this is the case, it's important to take a look at why you are working in a program that has a philosophy so different from yours. It's not okay to tell parents you disagree with the program's policies, because it's not fair to put parents in the middle of a disagreement between you and the rest of the staff. As an employee in a child care center, you must realize and accept your responsibility to carry out the philosophy, policies, and procedures of the center. You may need to think about whether it would be better for you to work in a program whose philosophy better matches your own. At the same time, consider the reasons the techniques listed earlier are inappropriate. The bottom line is that they don't work in the long run and they damage children. It is never okay for a child care program to use strategies that damage children to address a problem.

Helping the Parents of the Child Who Is Biting

When parents learn their child has bitten another child, their reaction can range from feelings of shock and guilt to accusations that the program is doing something wrong. It is important to work closely with parents so you and they can share information that may affect the biting. You will also want to let parents know what you are observing in the program and what responses you are trying.

Parents whose child was bitten and those whose child did the biting often say they felt more helpless when their child was the one who bit. You may need to offer as much support to these parents as you do to their children. Overall, you want to make sure that you and the parents are working together to end the biting, even though much of the specific work will be done in your program, because that is where the biting is occurring. If the biting is also occurring at home, you will want to work with parents to discover a likely cause and then develop a plan to work with the child consistently at child care and at home.

Parents may ask how they can help at home. Here are some suggestions:

▸ If you have a good idea of why you believe the child is biting, share the strategies and techniques related to those reasons with parents. They may be able to work on some at home. (Strategies and techniques are found on pages 36–43 in chapter 3.)

▸ If the parents are doing the innocent "play" biting described under "Imitation" on pages 11–12 in chapter 1, encourage them to replace it with some other affectionate behavior until the child is a little older.

▸ Help parents learn the importance of expressing disapproval for biting if the child bites at home. You may give them suggestions on doing this effectively, including appropriate tone of voice and wording. Help them understand that this does not mean lecturing, going off on a tirade, or punishing the child.

▸ Encourage parents to help their toddler develop language skills and to model appropriate ways to express feelings as well as caring and empathetic behavior.

Since many parents want to suggest punishments, you need to be prepared to explain just how valuable these actions will be for their child. Parents may imply that the fault lies with you or the program because their child "doesn't bite at home." Often this is the case, because many of the reasons toddlers bite are related to being around more people. Instead of reacting defensively, acknowledge that this may indeed be true and that the reasons their child is biting may be related to the group setting and the frustration that sometimes comes with it for toddlers.

Helping the Parents of the Child Who Is Being Bitten

Many programs report that this is one of the toughest jobs they have. Most parents react very strongly to biting. You can't assume that parents won't be furious with you if their child is bitten simply because you have previously had a good relationship with them. Even the most understanding, reasonable, knowledgeable parents can't help feeling a lump in their throat and a rising level of righteous rage when they see bite wounds on their toddlers. Sometimes it seems toddlers are bitten on the face more than any other part of the body; such bites appear not only painful but also disfiguring.

You need to recognize that the first response many parents have to biting is, "Where were you when this happened?" You may feel attacked, but such a question should not be entirely unexpected. Parents weren't there to protect their child, and to them it looks as if you weren't either. This is probably not the time to explain how very quickly toddlers can bite. Try responding with genuine regret as you tell them, "I wasn't where I could have stopped the bite. I feel terrible. I don't want any of the children to get bitten."

Here are some keys to an effective conversation with the parents of the child who was bitten:

▶ Acknowledge and respect the parents' feelings and the depth of those feelings.

▶ Tell them how you will help keep their child safe. This might include both increasing supervision and helping the child learn to stand up for herself. This helps the parent understand that you're not expecting the child to be responsible for her own safety, but you also do not want her to see herself as a victim.

▶ Tell them what you are doing to teach the child who bit not to bite anymore.

At this point, parents are likely to give suggestions, make demands, or issue ultimatums that you cannot accept. Be prepared for your efforts to go unappreciated by parents until the biting stops. You may be trying your very best, but parents are looking for results—often quick results. You can't stop the biting cycle as fast as they would like, which means you need to use all of your skills in working with families. Look to your program administrator for support.

Working with Parents of Other Children in the Program

When you're working with parents during biting episodes, most of your efforts will likely go toward the parents of the children directly involved. Parents of other children in the program, however, are almost certainly aware of what is happening and may also need some information and reassurance. You can help these parents in several ways.

First, make sure they know what you are doing to address the biting, and ask them to bring questions they have directly to you. Parents who feel they can get information and answers from you will be less likely to go to other parents to find out what they want to know. If you have developed a plan to deal with ongoing biting, all parents should have a copy of that plan and updates as the plan proceeds.

Second, tell them what you are doing to protect children from biting. This is especially important for parents of the youngest children in the group. These children may not be able to talk or get around as easily as older children, so parents may worry that these children will be easy targets for others who are biting. Let parents know you will tell them of any reactions their child may have to the biting in the room. Reassure them that you will comfort their child if he is upset by the biting. Ask them to share with you any reactions they notice in their child that they think may be related to the biting.

Finally, give them specific suggestions they can use at home with their own children. Advise them to follow their child's lead. If their child does not talk about the biting, they shouldn't pump the child for information. If their child tells them that a particular toddler is biting in their room, the parent can say, "I don't like biting, and Teacher Nancy doesn't like biting. Teacher Nancy will tell Adam, 'No biting!'"

If their child expresses concern that someone might bite him, parents can tell their child, "I don't want anyone to bite you. You can tell Adam, 'No biting!'" If the child seems quite worried, the parent can add, "We'll tell Teacher Nancy that you're worried, and she will help you."

Parents can also help their child learn words that label feelings, and they can model helping, empathetic behaviors for their child to imitate. Toddlers who can express their feelings and have experience with helping and empathy may be less likely to become participants in biting episodes; this may help reduce ongoing biting.

While these suggestions do not guarantee that children will never be bitten, they do help parents respond in a way that is reassuring and appropriate to their toddlers.

Sharing Success

You may want to have caregivers count and record the number of bites they intercept and prevent. This can help parents and staff alike recognize how their efforts are helping reduce the number of bites, and it can be especially useful if you have parents who are keeping their own running tally of the number of bites in your program. Keeping track of "saves" is a familiar practice; it is used in both hockey and soccer. Of course, the number of saves may not matter as much to parents as the number of bites, and you can't very well say, "Yeah, there were two bites today. But we had five saves, so it's okay." It's much more effective to say, "We did have two bites today, and that was upsetting. We're glad, though, that we were able to see five other bites coming and stop them before they happened." When people are counting, it's good to be able to recognize and acknowledge that saves count too. (Use this suggestion cautiously with parents, though. You don't want to antagonize them by focusing more on saves than on what is being done to stop the biting.)

When the Outside Community Is Aware of the Biting

Parents are not the only adults who have an interest in biting episodes at your program. You may occasionally find that the entire community seems to know that you have "a biting problem." Suddenly people who don't even have children in your program are talking about it at the grocery store, at work, and at community gatherings. It may seem that everyone is an expert on biting, giving opinions or passing judgment on your program and making pronouncements along the lines of "If *I* were in charge, I wouldn't allow biting in the first place—let me tell you!"

At one time, this was most likely to happen when parents talked to their friends and family about the biting and how the child care program was handling it. Now it also happens when parents use social media, complete with photos, to spread the news. And it spreads much farther and faster through social media than it ever did before. Of course, the people who are the most dissatisfied seem to talk and post the most. This can certainly hurt the reputation of your program and can also discourage staff. You can hardly issue a general gag order concerning the biting. Telling parents they are forbidden to talk about what is happening will certainly backfire and result in even less confidence in the program. It is likely to ensure that there will be even more negative comments about the program.

What you *can* do is try to create the message you *do* want the community to hear and then use every opportunity to get that message out. Your message needs to be genuine, positive, and engaging. It must also be true; that is, it must reflect what you really do.

Here is such a message: "Whenever we face challenges at the ABC Early Childhood Program, we work on them in ways that are appropriate for children, families, and staff. And we are willing to take the time to do it well." You can also use talking points, such as those in the next section, as brief, engaging messages that show your program in a positive light. Make sure you put the messages where people are most likely to see them. That starts with your social media accounts. You can also include these messages in letters, memos, and newsletters to families. Post them on bulletin boards. Some may work well in your program's parent handbook. Then, when people in the community ask questions or make comments about the "terrible biting" in the program, you can encourage staff to use your program's messages in their response.

This message should also be incorporated into the public relations work you do with the community. Do not wait for negative events or publicity and then issue defensive statements. Give the community an exciting, positive picture of your program on a regular basis. Write articles for community publications about what the children are doing in your program, and include pictures. Write informative articles for parents about child development. As you tell the community about your program, work in the message about how you handle problems.

Consider using parent testimonials as another way to present positive messages. When a biting situation has been resolved, see if there are parents who would be willing to give a short testimonial about how your program handled the biting. Ask parents to write out their testimonials and give written permission to let you post them on your social media accounts or use them in written communications for parents. Make sure the testimonials do not include the names of children involved. If you have a collection of these, you can keep them on reserve and use them as you choose.

Finally, we need to turn our attention to negative messages or details about specific biting episodes that may come from our own staff. All programs should have a section on confidentiality and professionalism in their staff handbook and perhaps in their employment policies. This should include both a general statement about confidentiality and professionalism as well as statements that refer to specific situations. One such statement should refer to expectations of professionalism and confidentiality during times when the program is working on difficult situations with children. Ongoing biting would certainly be one example. When the program is working on difficult situations, detailed information related to the situation is the responsibility of the program administrator and is not for staff to comment on outside of the program. Staff should not discuss the details of such situations outside of the program, either in conversation with others or through social media. It is appropriate for staff to use the program's messages and talking points about biting, but they should refrain from sharing details of specific biting situations. Of course, the administrator then must ensure that staff are familiar with the program's messages and talking points about biting. The administrator must also ensure that there is a plan to address the biting and that it is shared with staff and parents.

TALKING POINTS FOR COMMUNICATING ABOUT BITING

Talking points are statements that are compact, clearly expressed, and persuasive. They are, however, more than just concise messages; they are concise messages with an important purpose. When it comes to biting, we know many of the misconceptions people have. We also know many of the questions we are likely to face, often in a confrontational manner. Most of us find it difficult to respond when we're on the spot. We wish we had time to think through our response. Talking points are useful in situations like these when we want and need the right words and an effective tone to convey our message with a purpose. The talking points below are proactive statements based on the ideas and practices in *No Biting*. They are like a preemptive response to a question we know we'll be asked or a misconception we know is likely to come up. Using the talking points when we speak about biting, post to social media, or send out written material helps get our message out in front of the questions and misconceptions. This is so much better than waiting for them to arise and then being on the defensive. And, of course, these messages are very helpful when a question or misconception does arise, because the language and the tone we need are right there for us.

Below are several talking points that may be helpful to you in your communication with parents, staff, and other community members. The talking points can also be useful for study and discussion. You will almost certainly be able to identify the misconception or question each talking point was designed to address. Reflecting on the talking points using the following questions can help you identify the characteristics that make it effective. This can help you frame and develop your own talking points. Choose a talking point to examine in depth, and use these questions to guide you.

- ▶ What is it about the talking point that gets the issue out there, addresses it clearly, and conveys its purpose?

- ▶ How does the talking point convey the message without sounding patronizing, judgmental, or confrontational?

- ▶ What words or phrases seem especially effective?

- ▶ What do you notice about the language of the talking point? Why do you think the language of a talking point is important?

- ▶ What do you notice about the tone, the feel of the talking point? Why do you think the tone of a talking point matters?

Here are some talking points related to biting. They are in no particular order. They can be helpful to you in speaking about biting, but only if they reflect what you actually do in your own program.

- ▶ We know a lot about biting, and we've had our fair share of experience with it. But no matter how much we know or how much experience we may ever have, it always feels terrible when a child is bitten in our program. We will put all our energy into helping the children—the one who bit and the one who was bitten—but our first thought is always that we wish we could guarantee that biting would never happen. We know there is no such guarantee, but we can promise to put all our knowledge and experience to work on the biting so it stops.

- ▶ We take biting seriously here. When it comes to biting, there's a lot out there, so we had to decide what we would pay attention to and where we would get our information. Our work is based on *No Biting: Solutions and Support for*

Toddler Programs, a book written especially for early childhood programs. It was developed by toddler teachers who really know biting, and it was published by Redleaf Press. They specialize in books for programs just like ours. So, when it comes to biting, we have done our homework, and we know what to do.

▶ It is so tempting to think that toddlers bite for no reason. That would be pretty discouraging because there wouldn't be any way for us to help the child and stop the biting. Fortunately, there's always a reason; we just need to figure out what it is. To do this, we need to know the many reasons toddlers might bite—and we do. Then we observe the child to get some clues about which reason(s) might be behind the biting. And finally, once we have a good idea of why the child is biting, we know what kinds of strategies and techniques to use to help the child and stop the biting.

▶ When toddlers in our program bite, we don't use punishments. This may sound surprising, but there's a very good reason, and that is because we want the biting to stop. What we've learned (and what experts have learned as well) is that the best way to stop biting is to help toddlers calm down, let them know that biting is never the right thing to do, teach them what to do instead of biting, and make our toddler room and everything in our program a great match for the way toddlers develop, think, and learn. So that's what we do.

▶ The words *policies* and *biting* just don't seem like they belong together. And yet we have a biting policy, and we're glad we do. We took the time to learn about biting, to think about all the issues, and to decide what to do when it happens. This has turned out to be very helpful. Our policy steers us away from bad decisions, keeps everyone on the same page, and sets us on the best path for children.

▶ Wouldn't it be great if there was just a quick fix for biting? When it comes to biting, there's a lot of advice out there, so we'd all love that. We read about quick fixes; they're all over the internet. We hear about them because people suggest them to us. So we decided maybe we should check them out, and we did. Here's the problem. They are, indeed, quick. But they are not true fixes. They don't address the real cause of the biting, and they don't help the child who bit. We do care, and we will always help all the children when there is biting.

CHAPTER 5

Staff Members Working Together

During episodes of ongoing biting, parents are not the only adults who are under stress and perhaps feeling frustrated. The caregivers in the room also feel the pressure, because they are the ones who are trying to carry out the program, care for the toddlers, work with the parents, and stem the biting. To deal with biting effectively, toddler caregivers need information about biting, support from the administrator and other staff, resources to carry out a plan, and relief when necessary.

This book provides the information toddler caregivers need to understand biting and to choose responses that are likely to work. When biting becomes a repeated problem, they may need help from their administrator and other staff to develop a plan. Other teachers can help by serving as "fresh eyes" to observe the toddler room for program components that may be contributing to the biting. This is an important part of developing a plan to address ongoing biting, because caregivers who are in the room every day may not be able to see problems in the program.

Once a plan has been developed, toddler caregivers will certainly need the help and support of the program administrator and other teachers to implement it. The plan may call for a change in the room arrangement or the daily schedule, different or less equipment, additional materials, or even additional staff. Caregivers in the toddler program need to know how to request the help (or permission) they need to make these changes. They may need some physical help from other teachers to rearrange the room or remove equipment. If part of the plan involves additional staff, toddler caregivers need to know that the staff member joining them sees this assignment as a problem-solving opportunity rather than a punishment.

Toddler caregivers need to know that they can count on their coworkers not only for help with tasks but also for moral support as they take on biting. Without going into great detail, the program administrator should let all staff know what is happening. This can be as simple a statement as "Room 3 is working hard to deal with a rash of biting. They have developed a plan they will be trying over the next two weeks, and they need support from all of us. Please see me if you would like to help."

Other staff can help by asking how the plan is progressing and offering to listen with a sympathetic ear. They can also help by knowing how to respond to parents who complain to them about the biting and how it's being handled. It is quite likely that parents of toddlers in the room with the biting problem also have older children in the program. Some parents may try to draw the teachers of their older children into a discussion of the biting. This is the time for those teachers to support their colleagues in the toddler room by stating their confidence in the toddler caregivers and the plan they developed. They should direct the parents to speak directly with the teachers in the toddler room or with the program administrator. If other staff have concerns about how the biting is being handled, they owe it to the program to take those concerns to the administrator directly and privately.

Caregivers who are doing the hard work of addressing biting need to know where they can express their frustration and how they can get some relief from time to time. This is more difficult than it may seem. Stressed caregivers cannot just leave the room and take a break whenever they feel like it, because toddlers must be supervised and ratios must be maintained. Other staff cannot just trot in and out of the room all day to provide breaks; toddlers thrive on consistency and often fall apart when there are too many changes.

Programs may have to look for creative solutions to the problem of giving breaks to teachers stressed out by the biting. Is there any period during which having other staff in the room might be minimally disruptive to toddlers? For example, other teachers or a floater might be able to fill in for short periods during naptime. Administrators might use this break time to meet with caregivers and give them an opportunity to talk about how they are feeling, how the plan is working, and what additional help they need. Administrators can also provide some relief by being in the classroom to talk with parents at pickup time, which can be an overwhelming time of the day for caregivers.

Finally, if everybody in the program knows about the biting problems in the toddler room, then everybody ought to be told whenever there is measurable success. Administrators should publicize the good news, and other staff should offer sincere congratulations.

The Role of the Program Administrator

The program administrator plays a crucial role in addressing biting. She develops policies, supports staff, conducts staff development, communicates with parents, and sets the tone for the program. These are all crucial when a program is struggling with biting. During a biting episode, the administrator has a number of responsibilities, including

- making sure program policies related to biting are being followed;

- supporting teachers, giving them suggestions, and allowing them to vent their frustrations in private;

- providing appropriate staff development on biting;

- knowing where to find additional information, authorities, and technical assistance to deal with difficult biting problems;

- being available to serve as an observer in a classroom struggling with ongoing biting;

- being available to help develop plans to address ongoing biting;

- monitoring progress in implementing the plan;

- acknowledging staff efforts to deal effectively with biting and congratulating staff when biting subsides;

- offering appropriate information and resources to parents regarding biting;

- being available to help staff talk with parents who are upset or frustrated;

- taking the lead in developing messages related to the biting for parents and the community.

Because biting is not unexpected, and because it can be very difficult for everyone, program administrators need to think ahead of time about how to deal with biting when it occurs. It is much easier to develop policies that make sense for children, families, and the program when you are not in the middle of the stress and frustration of an ongoing string of biting incidents. The problem is easier to address when policies have already been decided and an action plan is ready for implementation. In addition, when staff have specific training about biting, they will be more effective in preventing and responding to it. Parents who have seen a biting policy in enrollment materials or in a parent handbook also are better prepared when biting occurs. All of this means that when you have policies in place before an outbreak of biting, the biting episode is likely to be less stressful for everyone involved. It will probably be less severe, end sooner, produce less friction between parents and staff, and thus be much easier on the program and the children.

Biting and plans to deal with it are important areas for staff development in toddler programs. Topics should include

- ▸ describing the program's philosophy and how it guides the program's policy on biting;

- ▸ reviewing toddler development;

- ▸ understanding the many different reasons toddlers bite;

- ▸ examining how the classroom environment affects biting;

- ▸ responding appropriately and effectively to biting;

- ▸ documenting biting incidents;

- ▸ observing toddlers;

- ▸ creating plans to address biting based on observations;

- ▸ talking with parents about biting.

Staff development seminars give toddler caregivers the opportunity to consider and discuss their feelings about biting. The behaviors we use with children come from our attitudes, beliefs, and perceptions. If we are having trouble implementing (or even imagining) appropriate responses to biting, we may need to start by working on our attitudes, beliefs, and perceptions.

Resources for Staff Orientation and Training

Directors have specifically asked for a curriculum based on *No Biting* to orient and train their staff. This is encouraging because it indicates that they've found the information in the book to be valuable. In our directors' focus group for this third edition, we decided that a ready-to-use curriculum based on *No Biting* and organized into short modules would work best. With individual modules, directors can work within a variety of time frames. With a fully developed curriculum, directors will be able to offer the modules easily and might ask experienced, trusted staff to help conduct the sessions. To meet this need, I created a user-friendly, fully developed staff training curriculum organized into eight modules. Each module has a simple one-page handout. You will find this curriculum in appendix D and also available as a web resource.

Directors have also asked for role-playing activities to help staff practice communicating with parents about biting situations. Role playing can be beneficial because participants have the opportunity to take the perspective of another person and to practice formulating appropriate responses. Role playing can also be difficult because many people hesitate or even decline to participate; they don't like being put on the spot. And sometimes role playing goes off course because a participant may create an exaggerated character who is unreasonable and unpredictable. To address these potential problems, I suggest a variation on traditional role playing. This variation along with complete directions and details is in appendix E and also available as a web resource.

When staff are in the throes of a difficult biting situation, they often need emotional support, encouragement, and help to work on it. Supporting staff during such times and in such ways is one of the most important aspects of a director's work.

Staff need someone to hear them and to acknowledge their emotions about the biting. They may feel distraught, frustrated, guilty, responsible, anxious, worried, confused, or pressured at this time. Directors need to take the time to listen without trying to move on to possible solutions too quickly. Teachers need to hear that someone understands the situation and has sympathy for them.

Staff also need to know that they are not alone in experiencing toddler biting. A director reported that one of her teachers was so relieved to know about *No Biting*. For this teacher, it wasn't the information in the book that was important; it was the mere fact that the book existed. It meant that biting was such a big problem for so many teachers, there was a whole book about it! She was not the only one with this struggle; it couldn't be all her fault. This can be the very relief some staff need to be able to move on to possible solutions.

Directors can then help staff focus on practices to address the biting based on how much and what kind of help teachers need. Directors may review with staff the process of deciding how to respond to the biting and turn the work over to them. Or they may work more directly with teachers to review observations, analyze the situation, consider strategies and techniques, and/or decide what to try. The key here is to give staff information and encouragement and to offer direct help when it is needed. Some directors call on experienced, trusted toddler caregivers to provide this direct help.

Staff may need additional observations of children or their classrooms; this is an excellent opportunity for the director to observe firsthand with a fresh set of eyes. The director must be able to devote time to such an observation, and this may require some schedule rearrangement. Such an observation might also be a task that can be delegated to a trusted, experienced toddler caregiver. Finally, directors can facilitate discussions to review observations and consider next steps. Making the time and taking the time to spend with teachers when biting occurs sends a powerful message that the director is able and willing to help her teachers when the going is difficult.

Administrators also need to prepare parents for the possibility of biting. This is a little more difficult than preparing staff, because you can hardly send parents a letter telling them to expect their child to be bitten in your program. What you *can* do is incorporate biting information in a memo or handbook that welcomes parents who are new to the toddler program. This memo or handbook should contain information on many aspects of the program, such as activities, schedule, staff, and so on. The information you provide on biting should focus on the specific steps your program takes when biting occurs. Specifics become very important to parents when their child has been bitten. The steps should, of course, reflect the decisions and plans you made as a staff. Developing this biting information for parents is important because it makes you review the steps you take and consider how these steps would sound to parents. Although we urge you to develop an information sheet that reflects your own decisions and plans concerning biting, a sample letter is offered in appendix A to help you get started.

CHAPTER 6

Developing Policies
about Biting

It is certainly tempting to wonder whether it's really necessary to have formal policies about biting in child care programs. The problem with not having policies is that when biting occurs, we do not have a position from which to address it. We are operating in a default mode: we haven't really thought about the issue or come to any understanding about it. When we are faced with a situation related to the issue, we end up doing whatever occurs to us at the moment. Our actions, then, are likely to be very inconsistent. In addition, if someone exerts pressure on us one way or the other, our actions are much more likely to go in the direction of that pressure. This is not a very comfortable position to be in, and certainly not a very professional one. It does a disservice to the children, families, and staff in the program.

Some programs have a policy that simply states they will deal with biting on a case-by-case basis. This is really a nonpolicy, because the programs are not taking, planning to take, or able to take any actions until after biting has happened. While in some situations we truly can't take any action until after something occurs, we can reasonably anticipate biting and can therefore plan our response to it. We can expect it will be potentially quite emotionally charged, and the way we deal with it will be very involved. A nonpolicy does not prepare us for any of this. Consider this analogy from another profession:

Firefighters certainly have to wait until there's a fire before they can react to it. However, they don't wait around until there's a fire to begin planning how they will fight it. They take a proactive stance and prepare for reacting to fires: they order equipment, participate in training, practice, develop policies and procedures, test their equipment, and much more.

73

We don't have to operate from a default mode. We can choose instead to operate from a decisive mode. This means we have given thought to an issue and have come to some understanding about it. This becomes our perspective. We then use that perspective to make a conscious decision about how we will approach situations related to the issue. These are our policies—the foundations on which our practices are built. Practices based on well-thought-out decisions are much more likely to be appropriate for children, families, and staff—including ourselves. However, we can't make good decisions without that foundation.

Perspective ➡ Policies ➡ Practices

Policy Components

Written policies that are clear and well thought out help ensure that biting will be dealt with appropriately and consistently by staff. These policies can also serve as a basis for discussing parents' concerns and suggestions. If a single agency or owner operates several early childhood programs, one policy should be used consistently in all the programs. Include the following in your policies on biting:

An introduction stating the program's perspective on biting. The way the program views biting sets the stage for everything else it does related to biting. Program staff who take the time to think carefully about biting are likely to develop, choose, and implement effective strategies to address it successfully.

How staff respond to biting. Your policy should state how staff will respond to individual biting incidents as well as to episodes of ongoing biting. You may choose to use a general statement, such as "Our staff express strong disapproval of biting. They work to keep the children safe and help the child who bit learn different, more appropriate behavior. When we have episodes of ongoing biting, we develop a plan of specific strategies, techniques, and timelines to address it. This plan is shared with all parents in the group." This part of the policy may also include specific actions that are prohibited when responding to biting. For example, you may want to add a sentence such as this: "Because we want the biting to stop as quickly as possible, we don't use techniques that alarm, hurt, or frighten children, such as biting back or washing a child's mouth out with soap."

How parents are informed about biting. Your policy should detail the procedure for informing parents about biting, including any special procedure for the parents of the child who bit and the parents of the child who was bitten. It should also include procedures for informing all parents when there is ongoing biting serious enough to warrant an action plan in the program.

How biting is documented. Your program should require that all incidents of biting be documented using the program's standard incident report forms. Make sure all staff are familiar with completing these forms, making them available to parents, and filing a copy with the program administration. If your program does not have such forms, see the examples in appendix C.

The role of confidentiality. Your policy should include what information concerning biting is kept confidential. Most often, this applies to the name of the child who bit or is biting. The reason for this confidentiality is that we do not want children labeled on the basis of only one of their behaviors. As discussed earlier, it is unfortunately very common to hear a child called "a biter." Remember that being labeled *a biter* defines the child in a negative way and makes it more difficult to work quickly and positively toward stopping the biting. In addition, parents may take it on themselves to chastise the child who bit their child or to try to punish that child's parents. Confidentiality is a cornerstone of professionalism in the early childhood field. You cannot practice selective confidentiality and still expect to build trusting relationships with parents.

What first aid is given for biting. First aid for biting should be based on medical advice and an understanding of the risk of infection. You can use the information on pages 21–22 to develop and communicate your own policies.

A sample policy for you to refer to when developing your own policy can be found in appendix A.

What about a "Three Bites and You're Out" Policy?

Some directors, staff, and parents want to have a policy that expels children from the program after a certain number of bites. This seems logical and fair to many adults. The idea is similar to the "three strikes and you're out" laws currently in effect around the country. This approach has many problems as a policy to address biting.

What underlies such a policy is a belief that toddlers are solely responsible every time they bite and that they can make conscious, informed decisions not to bite. We know, however, that many factors can contribute to biting, and not all of them are within the child's control. The environment, for example, is the caregivers' responsibility. If the biting were the direct result of an inappropriate environment, would anyone suggest there be a "three bites and you don't have to pay for a week of child care" policy or a "three bites and the teacher gets fired" policy?

The goal of this kind of exclusion policy is not to help the toddler learn different, more appropriate behavior but to eliminate children from the program when they don't behave in acceptable ways. The problem is that all toddlers behave in unacceptable ways some of the time—that's part of how they learn how to do what is acceptable. Like all learning, this is a slow, two-steps-forward one-step-back process. When you have a policy like "three bites and you're out," caregivers no longer focus on helping toddlers but rather on counting bites. It puts caregivers in a terrible position, because this policy is legalistic in nature, and legalistic approaches create legalistic complications.

For example, what should actually count as a bite? Caregivers may have an eagle eye out for the third bite from a child who is difficult to work with. As soon as teeth are bared, the third bite is recorded, and the child has to leave because "that's our policy." For a child who is in better graces, adults may decide not to count a bite that "wasn't really a bite; it was just a little nip." Sometimes biting happens, and no one sees it. Must a child be "charged" with the bite? And isn't it likely that a child who has been biting will be the chief suspect?

Caregivers and parents may also decide that there is such a thing as "a justified bite." If a child bites because another child hit him, should that bite count?

What happens when there is a discrepancy in the bite count? A teacher or caregiver may insist a child has reached the magic number of bites, but a parent is sure the child still has one more to go.

Furthermore, what is the time frame for counting these bites? Three bites in a day? Three bites in a week? Three bites in a month? Is there a statute of limitations so if a child doesn't bite for two months, his previous bite record is erased and he starts over? Does the bite count go with him to the next toddler room?

We know that about half of children bite during the toddler years. A "three bites and you're out" policy might create a contingent of "wandering toddlers" who go from one program to another in which the same thing could happen. Instead of responsive, consistent care, the toddler might endure a series of short-term child care experiences. This, of course, would put more stress on the child, increasing the chance that he would bite, while limiting the opportunity for him to learn from stable, loving caregivers how to behave differently.

Toddlers might not be the only victims of this policy. It could also hurt the program it was designed to protect. Enrollment could suffer because parents who must take their toddler out of a program would most likely take older siblings out too. Moreover, teachers would not be working on developing the skills and creating the environments that effectively address biting. These skills and environments enhance the overall quality of the program and benefit all the children, not just those who are biting.

Biting as a Reason to Exclude Children

Should biting be a reason to exclude a child from your program? This is a touchy subject because it is a frequent request, demand, or even ultimatum from parents. Anyone who has been a director for any length of time has heard something to the effect of "Either you kick that biter out, or I'm pulling my child out of here." When faced with such an ultimatum, it is certainly tempting to solve the problem by expelling the child who is biting. This may be especially true when you risk losing several families. It may seem like a simple solution to a complicated problem.

It is not, however, a simple solution. Let's consider the program implications first. A program that expels a child for biting is indicating either that it doesn't know enough to work on the problem or that it is unwilling to work on the problem—or both! A program that considers itself lacking the knowledge, skill, and motivation to deal with biting is most likely going to lack knowledge, skill, and motivation in its work with children. Is this what we are offering parents and children? When we do the hard work of acquiring knowledge, developing skills, and providing the best for children, our programs become stronger and more appropriate for children and families. When we excuse ourselves from doing this, our programs become weaker. Programs that have actively, painfully, and successfully addressed biting do not use biting as a reason to exclude children. And they often lose very few families as a result of their policies.

Let's also consider the child who is biting and her family. When a child is biting repeatedly, she needs help to learn other, more appropriate behavior from adults she knows and trusts. This is the most likely way to stop the biting. But it can't happen if she goes from program to program, from adults she knows and trusts to adults who are strangers. Parents may feel they must either avoid or lie about the reason for leaving the previous program when they try to enroll their child in a new one. As a result, they can't get the help and support they need.

Programs often claim to be justified in expelling a child for biting because they have "tried everything." When programs call Child Care Solutions with this statement, it usually turns out that "everything" has been a short list of approaches—some appropriate and some not—tried once or twice each. We urge programs to try the approaches in this book consistently for several weeks. While this will require more effort, that effort is likely to pay off.

Sometimes a Child Should Leave the Program

As committed as most caregivers are to the children and families in their programs, a few children do need a different kind of setting to stop biting. This is determined after trying all other approaches consistently over time. Most likely, biting is not the only problem the child is having in the program. In such a case, your program should review what it has tried and perhaps ask for outside help in this review. If you conclude that the needs of the child are beyond what even a good program—one with knowledge, skill, and motivation—can provide, you must face the possibility that this child might need a different kind of setting or program. Sometimes, for example, a very sensitive child is too overwhelmed by a large infant-toddler program and really needs the smaller group size and multiage character of a good family child care home. This admission comes with regret. When this happens, you need to provide support to the child's parents. Make sure you know how to refer the parent to other resources to find appropriate care for their child. You can start with your local child care resource and referral agency.

Biting and HIV/AIDS

Parents and caregivers may express concern over transmission of HIV/AIDS through biting and may even cite it as a reason to exclude a child who is biting. To respond to these concerns, it is important that we have accurate, up-to-date information about HIV/AIDS transmission. For the first edition of this book, our original task force contacted a local organization, AIDS Community Resources, for such information. The information they provided us was based on a 1994 statement from the federal Centers for Disease Control and Prevention (CDC). AIDS Community Resources urged child care programs and providers to stay up to date in their knowledge of HIV/AIDS transmission by using the CDC as their primary source of information. We have taken their advice, contacting the CDC for the second edition of *No Biting* and again now for this third edition.

Using the CDC's HIV/AIDS hotline, I was able to speak directly with a representative about HIV transmission as it relates to toddler biting. She directed me to the CDC's webpage specifically devoted to how HIV/AIDS is and is not transmitted. On this webpage, "HIV Transmission," the CDC states that "in extremely rare cases HIV has been transmitted by being bitten by a person with HIV. Each of the very small number of documented cases has involved severe trauma with extensive tissue damage and the presence of blood. There is no risk of transmission if the skin is not broken." None of these cases involved children. Blood-to-blood contact with severe trauma and extensive tissue damage would be very unusual among toddlers.

Still, parents may be concerned about saliva. According to the same webpage from the CDC, "HIV isn't transmitted through saliva."

Early childhood programs and providers can monitor this webpage, "HIV Transmission," regularly. It uses a question-and-answer format and is updated often. It is available at www.cdc.gov/hiv/basics/transmission.html. The CDC's HIV Hotline number is 800-232-4636 (800-CDC-INFO). There is also a Spanish language hotline at 800-344-7432 and a TTY line at 800-243-7889.

Documenting Biting

All bites should be documented on the forms your program uses for incidents. Using these forms for biting is an indication to parents that your program takes biting seriously and that you are not trying to hide biting incidents. Incident forms also help address the problem that arises when the teacher who is with the child at pickup time is not the teacher who was in the program when the bite occurred. These forms may also be useful when looking at biting patterns, because they contain specific information about time, place, and circumstances of the biting.

Because biting understandably stirs strong emotions in parents, an incident form left in the child's cubby for the parent to discover may be seen as uncaring. You need to tell parents face-to-face about the biting. Your words, tone, and body language should convey genuine regret that their child was bitten. Giving parents this news is not easy, and parents consistently tell us they want caregivers to be as upset about the bite as they are and to take it as seriously as they do. After parents have had the chance to make sure their child is all right, you can give them the incident form.

Most programs have their own incident forms already in place. We have included three sample forms in appendix C if you need a template or want to revise the form your program currently uses. If you have a choice, we suggest using an incident report instead of an accident report. Reporting the bite as an "accident" may be inflammatory to parents who insist "This was no accident. It was deliberate!"

CHAPTER 7

Consultation and
Technical Assistance for Biting

The early care and education field now includes specialists who provide training, consultation, and technical assistance to infant and toddler programs. They respond to requests from programs that need help with specific situations, and it's not surprising that this often revolves around biting. Such requests were the very reason this book was first created. When programs are struggling with biting, sometimes a short consultation is all that's needed. But often the program needs more comprehensive consultation and a great deal of technical assistance.

The goal of this longer-term consulting and technical assistance is to help programs address their specific biting situations effectively and appropriately. This chapter is devoted to helping specialists provide high-quality consulting and technical assistance on biting and is based on *No Biting*. It begins with a perspective on consulting and the knowledge and skills required for conducting consultation and technical assistance. It identifies consulting components and outlines a process to structure this work. It provides specific information on the consulting components and follows up with real-life examples. Finally, it includes questions for reflection and skill building related to the examples for each component.

A Perspective on Consulting

Just as the information on biting in this book begins with a perspective on biting, this process begins with a perspective on consulting. It is important because the work we do and the *way* we do that work always comes from the way we *view* the work. Here is a perspective that guides our thinking and our actions so we can provide effective, appropriate consulting and technical assistance:

▶ Biting in early childhood programs is a complicated matter, evoking strong emotions and putting great pressure on staff, directors, and parents.

▶ Early childhood programs are caught in the customer service dilemma that results when doing what is right for children may not be popular with parents who are the customers.

▶ Staff and directors come to the consulting process with a wide range of perspectives, knowledge, skill, and experience related to biting.

▶ We meet staff and directors where they are, acknowledging their current perspectives, and we work as respectful partners to increase their understanding of biting, their confidence, and their skills to address it.

▶ Staff and directors need high-quality information about biting, insights into their particular biting situations, and appropriate, practical suggestions. That is what we offer.

▶ All progress counts.

Knowledge and Skills for Consulting and Offering Technical Assistance on Biting

The consulting and technical assistance model in this chapter is built on the content of *No Biting*, so it is vital that specialists are thoroughly familiar with it. As we consult and offer technical assistance, we will need

▶ an appropriate perspective on biting;

▶ a solid understanding of biting;

▶ knowledge of the many reasons young children might bite and how to discern them;

▶ knowledge of specific practices that help reduce biting related to these reasons;

▶ the ability to observe children and classrooms for insight into and analysis of specific biting situations, and the ability to use the results to identify strategies to address the biting;

▶ the ability to communicate—both listen and speak—with staff and directors;

▶ the ability to develop, communicate, implement, and evaluate plans to address biting;

▶ the ability to guide directors in creating policies related to biting; and

▸ the ability to help directors and teachers communicate with parents about biting.

The Consultation / Technical Assistance Process

Here is a process that is comprehensive and purposeful. It is designed for in-depth work on biting situations and, as such, is done over time. It includes all the people who are involved in the situation. This chapter includes detailed information on each step in this process:

1. Consultants conduct an effective intake interview to respond to requests for help with biting and to provide consultation / technical assistance related to the specific request.

2. Consultants structure and conduct observations of children, classrooms, and programs as needed to gain information and insights into specific biting situations.

3. Consultants communicate and conduct effective meetings with caregivers, administrators, and parents as needed to share observations, insights, and information; to elicit information and insights from them; and to build consensus around action steps to address the biting.

4. Consultants use information from the observation and the meeting(s) with caregivers, administrators, and parents to craft and present a plan to address the specific biting situation that is developmentally appropriate for the child; doable for the caregivers; and supportive for the families. Consultants are available to demonstrate specific techniques for caregivers.

5. Consultants work with caregivers and administrators to develop an implementation plan and to measure progress and ensure that changes and improvements are sustained.

HOW MIGHT THIS PROCESS WORK IN PRACTICE?

Here is a chronology of this process in a real-life consultation for the Toddler Rainbow Room:

▸ **February 17.** Contact from a program director for help with ongoing biting by several children in a toddler room, especially a boy named Ryan, who has bitten the most.

▸ **March 2.** Meeting with the director to discuss the biting situation in the Rainbow Room and to talk about the consulting process. We agreed to proceed.

▶ **March 3.** Email contact with director about sitting down with teachers to listen to their concerns and ideas about the biting. After checking with teachers and arranging for coverage, she emailed back a date.

▶ **March 6.** Classroom observation in the Rainbow Room.

▶ **March 7.** Meeting with teachers to get their observations, thoughts, and insights. Following the meeting, I developed my ideas, my plan, and suggestions. I wrote this up as a report.

▶ **March 8.** Meeting (half an hour) with director to discuss report. Meeting with teachers (hour and a half) to present and discuss report. The report incorporated their observations, thoughts, and insights along with my observations and suggestions.

▶ **March 15.** Meeting with teachers to help them develop a plan to address the biting based on the suggestions in the report.

▶ **March 17.** Emailed director with results of the conversation with teachers.

▶ **March 22.** Follow-up conversation with director.

▶ **March 29.** Email Ryan's parents to set up a meeting and to express their thoughts.

▶ **April 6.** Meeting with Ryan's parents.

▶ **April 20.** Follow-up conversation with director on progress.

Putting the Process to Work

What follows is an in-depth look at each step of the consulting process. For each one, you will find background information, specific suggestions, examples from real consultations with toddler programs, and exercises to build consulting skills.

CONDUCTING THE INTAKE INTERVIEW

Most longer-term consultations begin with contact from an early childhood program director requesting help with a biting situation. This call often comes at a point where everyone in the program is feeling overwhelmed and frustrated. They almost always report that they've been working on the biting situation for some time and are not seeing any progress. Often they have tried one technique after another, rather like hanging individual pieces of clothing on a clothesline. The clothesline may be full of pieces of clothing, but nothing really hangs together! This initial call gives us great insight into what the director and staff perceive is happening and how they feel about it. While we may want to jump in and offer our thoughts and suggestions during this initial call, we will learn more and be more effective in the long term if we listen first.

Here are suggestions for this initial interview:

▶ This is a time to listen.

▶ Put the perspective to work. Listen for and accept the emotion, frustration, and current understanding of biting the caller expresses.

▶ Listen for the information the caller gives and then backfill specifics as needed. It is important to give the caller the opportunity to present the situation in his or her own words at this point. Later in the call, you may need to ask for specific information, such as

- the name and date of birth of the child;

- the length of time the child has been in the current classroom and in the center (if those are different);

- how long the biting has been going on (number of days, weeks, and so on);

- details about the classroom, such as the number of children and teachers, the age range of the children in the room, and so on.

▶ Listen for indications of perspective, knowledge, and skills related to biting and feelings about the child, parents, teachers, and the situation. Ask open questions to elicit more information if needed. Here are some examples:

- "What have you noticed about how teachers and other children relate to him?"

- "What have you tried so far?"

- "Have you had any conversations with his parents? If so, what were those like?"

▶ Resist the temptation to begin analyzing or speculating at this point.

▶ Ask the caller, "What do you hope will come out of our work together?" or "If this works really well, what will be different?" This moves the conversation to the point of talking about positive outcomes, which sets the stage for an effective consultation.

▶ Present the consultation process and talk with the caller to determine whether the program is ready to work in this way. You may hear or sense that the program has already decided to expel a child and is requesting the consultation to get your agreement or approval. In such an instance, it is fair and prudent to ask, "Have you already made a decision about this child?" The goal of this kind of consultation never includes rubber-stamping a program's decision to expel or "disenroll" a child. It is possible that, after careful observation, consultation, and work in the classroom, you may believe that the child will not be able to remain in the program. But we do not come to this conclusion quickly or easily. Be honest with the caller that the goal of this consultation process is to help the program help the child stop biting.

SKILL PRACTICE WITH A SAMPLE INTAKE INTERVIEW

Late yesterday the LMNOP Child Care Center called you and left a message on your voice mail saying that they need help with biting. It is first thing this morning, and you have just called back. Here is what the director tells you.

"Oh, thank goodness you called me back! We're at the end of our rope here over this biting. Our little guy is twenty-two months old, and he has been biting for about two months. He bites just about everyone in the room, and what's really puzzling is that he doesn't seem to care when he bites. He doesn't try to run away or anything. It's actually pretty amazing that he can even bite anyone with all the things he has in his mouth all the time. We have two brand-new teachers in that room, and they have never dealt with biting before. They have tried everything—time out, making him hold the ice on the children he bites, and telling him that teeth are for food— but he's still biting. The teachers try to tell him to use his words, but he doesn't really talk much yet. He knows lots of words and he understands every single thing you say to him, but he doesn't really make sentences yet the way some of the older kids in the room do. The only time he doesn't bite is when he's outside or when he has his binkie. The teachers are hanging in there, but it's getting so hard. The other children run away when he comes near them, and he looks so sad when that happens. The poor little guy! The teachers worry that they are not being consistent because when he's upset, they hold him and hug him. But they feel that if they are too nice to him, he will think that he's being good, and when he bites, he's not. They really want to do the right thing, but they don't know what that is!

"His parents feel terrible and want suggestions for what they can do at home, but I truly don't know what to tell them. So far the other parents are being pretty understanding, but I don't know how long that can last. We tell them all the things we're trying, but they can see that nothing is working. Our teachers are just desperate for some ideas about what's going on and to find out if there's anything that might help."

Here are questions to help you reflect and build skills related to conducting the initial interview. What do you feel this call reveals

- ▸ about the director's perspective on biting?

- ▸ about the director's knowledge and skills related to biting?

- ▸ about the caregivers' knowledge and skills related to biting?

- ▸ about the director's feelings toward the child, parents, caregivers, and the situation?

What questions might you want to ask for further insights into this situation?

OBSERVING CHILDREN AND CLASSROOMS

It is important for the specialist to observe the child in the classroom for two reasons. First, that's where the child has been biting. You can see how the child interacts with the classroom environment, with other children, and with caregivers. Second, you are observing with a fresh set of eyes, a solid understanding of toddler development, and specific knowledge about biting. Sometimes teachers worry that the child might not bite during your observation. This is understandable because they think you might not believe that the child actually bites or that you won't be able to learn anything about the biting unless you actually see a bite. However, this observation sets the stage for you to learn about the child, to gain some insights into possible reasons for the biting, and to ask questions of caregivers for more information and clarification.

The type of observation I have found to work best for this resembles a transcription of a short video. Whatever actions, behaviors, or facial expressions you would see on the video are written down. Whatever sounds, words, or conversation you would hear on the video are there in words. Even details about the background are written down. Because it is a written account of what you actually saw and heard, it is usually very recognizable to teachers. They realize that you saw what they experience. This helps everyone start out on the same page when it comes to understanding what might be at the root of the biting.

When observing, don't worry about sentence structure or even complete statements. Descriptive phrases are fine. Put any questions that occur to you in the margins to ask teachers about later. Also jot down any insights you might have as you observe.

Here is a sample observation of a child from a consultation in my own experience. It is here just as I wrote it at the time. You'll see mostly complete sentences but also some incomplete ones. The names of the children, the teachers, the center, and the classroom have been changed.

SAMPLE OBSERVATION OF A CHILD

Observation of Jackson R.   Date: May 5, 2012   Age: 28 months

Toddler II Room at the ABC Early Childhood Center   Observer: Gretchen Kinnell

Teachers: Melody (head teacher), Tasha (assistant teacher), Kim (floater)

Children: five girls, four boys present (one boy, Eddie, was not present) all between 28 months and 36 months

9:35   **All children engaged in circle time. Melody was leading.**

- Jackson sitting on Tasha's lap, sitting back against her. Children all listening to Melody read a book. Jackson spontaneously leaned forward, smiled, and yelled, "Roar!" when Melody read the word *lion*. Then leaned right back against Tasha.

- Jackson covered his eyes and lowered his head to decline participating in individual "clothes" song, which called for children to come forward individually and included jumping. He participated in group songs, smiling but not doing the motions. During the songs he became more animated, leaning forward.

- Did not participate in "jumping ABCs" song. Tasha stood him up, but he immediately plopped back into her lap. Repeated this twice.

- At every opportunity, he made "pop" noises and "scream" noises at the end of songs. He showed great delight—clapping his hands, smiling, becoming more animated—each time he did this.

9:50   **Art project—all children did this; they were divided between two tables.**

- Jackson watched what other children were doing, then colored his own paper stocking. He put cotton balls on the top of the paper stocking, which the teacher had spread with glue. He did this very slowly, with great care and deliberation, placing each one and pushing it down on the glue.

- As children finished, they went to play in various areas of the room. Jackson brought three crayons over to the table that had two large sheets of paper on it. He showed me the crayons, then became aware of a small speck of cotton on his fingertip. He slowly worked on taking it off, trying several times to get it off. He was very careful and intent as he held up his finger, looked at it intently, and used his thumb and pointer finger to remove it. After several attempts he was successful.

- Jackson sat next to a little girl, Lucy, at this table and colored. He chattered to Tasha, who sat next to him. The chattering did not contain any specific or intelligible words. His tone of voice was conversational. At one point, he colored off the paper and said very clearly, "Uh oh."

10:00	· Jackson got up from the table and played peekaboo with me, hiding behind Tasha. He laughed; his eyes were wide open and sparkling. He tried several ways to trick me into looking for him. Each time I saw him and said, "There he is!" Jackson laughed loudly. His laughter increased in volume, duration, and excitement as the game went on.
	· Jackson noticed a small lump of crayon that had come off on the paper—very small, but noticeable. He spent one minute looking at it intently, touching it and doing nothing else.
	· He got up from his chair and Lucy sat in it. "Chair," he told Tasha as he pointed to the girl in the chair he had just left. The word "chair" was intelligible. Tasha asked if he could sit with Lucy on the chair. He nodded and the two children sat together on the same chair, even though other seating options were available. Tasha asked if he wanted the chair she was sitting on. "No," he said (again the word was very clear). There were no problems with both of the children sitting in the same chair. Lucy seemed not to notice or care that Jackson was there; Jackson seemed not to notice or care that Lucy was so close by.
10:05	· Kim arrived, and Melody went on a break. Tasha took Melody's place supervising the larger area of the room. Kim took Tasha's place near the table with the coloring activity.
	· Kim sat in Tasha's chair. Kim stood up, and Jackson moved the chair closer to where he had been sitting with Lucy. "Are you moving my chair?" Kim asked him in a kind of teasing voice. He quickly let go of the chair and went back to the other chair. A moment later, he went to sit on Kim's chair, glanced at me, and shrugged his shoulders. It looked to me as if he were conveying the message that he had been "caught," then moved away from the chair.
10:15	· Jackson put a small toy whale in his mouth, sucked on it, and bit it. He took it out of his mouth when Kim asked him to, then put it back in and left it there for two minutes.
	· Very deliberately and carefully put small toy bears on a surface right at his eye level; he tried to put them on my book, but it didn't work. The book was too unstable, and the bears toppled over. He said, "Uh oh." I tapped the tabletop right next to me and said, "Try putting them here." He did it immediately.
	(Note: He responded very quickly and positively to what adults suggested, especially when combined with a visual cue.)
10:20	· He held out the little toy bear toward the other children and "roared" very loudly. Then he smiled. He came back to the coloring table. He turned over the crayon container so all the crayons (about twenty) rolled out. He put them all in the container, one by one. Then he repeated this.

10:25	• Jackson put the tiny toy teapot in his mouth and chewed on it. He took that out and put the baster in his mouth.
	• He played with large interlocking blocks. He started to climb on them. Kim said not to climb on them. She noted that these blocks are new. Kim and I commented that they did look like something you should climb on, especially as the children started to build with them. Kim then helped him sit in the structure as children built it up around him. He readily accepted sitting in the structure and stopped trying to climb on the blocks.
10:30	• He sought out Kim for her to pick him up. She did and he buried his head in her shoulder. She asked, "Are you okay?" He shook his head no and kept it buried in her shoulder. She asked him what was the matter, but he didn't respond, just kept holding on to her.
	(Note: I think Jackson used this strategy to regain control of himself. This lasted three minutes; then he got down.)
10:35	• He brought me a foam pegboard. I put a crayon in one of the holes so it stood up. He was fascinated and tried it himself. "I do," he said. He became very excited, doing it again and again. He became more and more excited, moving faster and breathing faster. Then he bit the foam pegboard.
10:45	**Getting ready to go outside.**
	• The children were putting on coats. Jackson was hanging on the handle of the door to the outside. Melody directed him away from the door handle; he complied readily.
	• He was very persistent in finding and putting away all the little plastic bears, looking under the cots to find the very last one.
	• He pointed and talked to other children. He pointed to the door and said clearly, "Mommy."
	• He immediately took the hand of the child next to him when directed to do so to get ready to go outside.
	(Note: He is a great imitator. We could take advantage of that by showing him what to do, doing it with him, and then letting him do it on his own.)
	(Note: No child showed any reluctance to be near him.)

Here are questions to help you reflect and build skills related to observing children:

▶ What specific observations of Jackson do you feel provide insights into his biting?

▶ Based on the observation, what occurs to you about possible reasons for Jackson's biting?

▶ What suggestions might you make to address his biting?

▶ What do you think it would be like for you to do a similar observation? Why do you think this?

Communicating and Meeting with Directors, Staff, and Parents

Throughout the consulting process, you will meet with caregivers, directors, and perhaps parents. Such meetings might be with caregivers alone, a director alone, parents alone, or some combination of these. Here are the most likely purposes for these meetings:

- ▸ to hear their observations and insights on the child(ren) and on the biting
- ▸ to share information, observations, and suggestions with them
- ▸ to work together to develop plans to address the biting
- ▸ to follow up on progress
- ▸ on rare occasions, to facilitate parent group meetings

These meetings are a crucial part of the consulting process. All our knowledge and skill in observing children, analyzing biting situations, and making suggestions become useless if we are not able to work effectively with the adults involved. This is why it's so important for us to make these meetings effective. We do this by listening to those we're meeting with, engaging them in the process, providing high-quality information and suggestions, and working with them as partners. Here are suggestions for effective meetings with teachers, directors, and/or parents.

SCHEDULING MEETINGS

Schedule all meetings with teachers through the director. When meeting with caregivers, you will need a space and time away from distractions. Be aware that scheduling time for meetings with caregivers in early childhood programs is often difficult because ratios and coverage require that other adults take their place. This often requires rearranging the schedules of other adults in the program. For all these reasons, it's important to respect the time frames the program is able to provide by ending on time and being well prepared for the meeting. Meetings will vary in length depending on the purpose for the meeting. If you are meeting with caregivers to hear their thoughts about the biting, even a solid half hour of meeting time will be valuable. If you feel you need more time, you might decide to schedule another meeting. If you are meeting with the caregivers to share your observations, insights, and suggestions, you will need a longer time period.

You will probably schedule meetings with individual parents directly; however, it's important for the director to know when you will be meeting with them. Meetings with parent groups should be set up and scheduled by the director.

PREPARING FOR MEETINGS

Come to the meeting with a purpose and present it clearly:

▶ "Today we are meeting to hear your [the caregivers'] observations and thoughts about the biting that you've been experiencing in the classroom."

▶ "In this meeting, we'll be reviewing and discussing suggestions for addressing the biting."

▶ "I appreciate being able to meet with you, Riley's caregivers and parents, to talk about what we can do at the center and at home to help and support him."

Come prepared for the meeting with appropriate questions, comments, and relevant materials. If the purpose is to hear from caregivers or parents, listen carefully and take notes. If the purpose is to share observations and suggestions, put them in writing and make copies for everyone attending the meeting. Give a copy to the director if he or she will not be at the meeting. Encourage caregivers to bring any notes or documentation they may have to share. The Biting Incident Documentation and Reflection Form in appendix C is especially useful for this.

DURING THE MEETING

Check in with teachers and parents. "As I talked about my observations of Ellie, does it sound like the Ellie you know?" If you share actual anecdotes from your observation, caregivers and parents are almost certain to feel that you have really seen the child. Choose anecdotes that show the child in a positive light. These might involve endearing behaviors such as giving another child a tissue to wipe her nose. You might note a strength of the child, such as his skill and care in block building. This helps create a positive relationship with caregivers and parents. You can also use the same approach with observations of classrooms. "So, when I talk about what I saw in your classroom, does that sound like your room?"

Listen for strong feelings. Offer understanding and empathy if caregivers or parents express frustration or anger; remember that biting often elicits strong emotions. Express your belief that the situation can get better and that this meeting is a good step toward that outcome. Also listen for misconceptions about biting. For example, someone may say, "Well, of course we all know that biting is aggression, pure and simple!" This is not true, and it is important that we clear up the misconception. But we really cannot respond with a statement that starts, "No, it's not . . . ," no matter how good the rest of the explanation is. This creates an argumentative air, and that will stand in the way of working effectively on the biting. Instead, you can use a gentle approach. "It sure can look like all biting is aggression, because the child who was bitten gets hurt. Sometimes it is aggression, but children also bite when they are worried or when they're overexcited. What we have to do is to figure out the reason for *this* biting. That's what will really help us come up with the best possible solution." Another way to gently challenge misconceptions is by starting with, "You know, it's tempting to think that . . ." Here's an example: "You know, it's tempting to think that if we make a child drink undiluted lemon juice when she bites, she'll figure out that she shouldn't bite. But the truth is that toddlers just won't make the connection between the biting and the lemon juice. And if they're biting because they are frustrated, it won't even matter if they *could* make that connection."

Pay attention to who speaks and who doesn't during the meeting. Elicit comments from those who may not be speaking much. "Allie, what are you seeing?" "Allie, how do you think this suggestion might work?" It's important for everyone to be heard, and it's important for you to hear everyone's comments, questions, and ideas.

ENDING THE MEETING

End the meeting with a short recap and talk about next steps. Include details about specific action steps. Write these details down and make sure everyone gets a copy. Thank everyone for their contribution to this work on the biting situation. End on a positive, hopeful note. "This has been a difficult situation, but now we have some ideas we've decided to try. Anytime we can move in this direction, that's progress!"

Here is an example of a short meeting with teachers. It relates to the consultation on Jackson's biting with the ABC Early Childhood Center's Toddler II room. I met with teachers shortly after my observation, but before I developed suggestions for Jackson's biting; we had a half hour for the meeting. I started the meeting with, "I'm glad you are able to meet today. I enjoyed being in your classroom yesterday. As I review and think about my observations, I'd really like to know what you have observed and what you think. After all, you are with him every day."

Teachers shared the following observations and thoughts:

▶ Tasha and Melody had read over the section in *No Biting* about reasons toddlers bite. They had wondered whether Jackson's biting may be related to oral-motor development. However, neither Tasha nor Melody feels that he puts things in his mouth any more than other children.

▶ Melody feels that he may bite when he gets overstimulated. She noted how easily he becomes overexcited. She also cited his lack of verbal language and possible teething.

▶ Melody noted that when all the children are there, Jackson is more likely to bite. (On the day I observed, there were a total of nine children in the room. Usually there are ten. The one boy who often "gets Jackson going" was not present during this observation.)

▶ They don't feel that the other children try to avoid Jackson; at the same time, Jackson doesn't usually seek out other children to play with.

The director had already made the arrangements for all of us to meet together the next day to go over my observations and suggestions. The director would make sure coverage was in place for the teachers. I'd make sure to have my observation and suggestions in written form and make copies for everyone.

We ended the meeting with the teachers expressing relief that maybe they were finally "going to get somewhere" with this biting situation.

Here are questions to help you reflect and build skills related to meetings with teachers, directors, and parents:

▶ What information, steps, and suggestions from "Communicating and Meeting with Directors, Staff, and Parents" can you identify in this sample meeting?

▶ In what ways do you feel the comments from the teachers can be useful to this consultation?

▶ What sense do you have of the teachers' engagement during this half-hour meeting? How did you come to your conclusion?

Developing and Presenting Plans and Suggestions

When you have spoken with caregivers to get their observations, thoughts, and insights and done your own observation in the classroom, you will likely have a great deal of information that relates to the biting situation. Take the time to carefully consider all the information and use it to develop insights into the biting. Use your insights to discern

▶ what may be causing and/or contributing to the biting,

▶ what may be helping the child already,

▶ whether there is a specific adult the child is especially close to and seeks out,

▶ whether there are activities or areas of the room the child especially seems to enjoy, and

▶ how the child and the other children in the room interact with each other.

This becomes the foundation for developing a plan to address the biting. Here is an example. It is based on my observation of Jackson and the meeting with his teachers mentioned above. It is the report I wrote and shared at a meeting with Melody, Tasha, and the director. Note that rather than rewrite specific suggestions that are already in *No Biting*, I referenced them and we reviewed them together in the meeting. The center already had a copy of the book.

OBSERVATIONS, THOUGHTS, AND SUGGESTIONS TO HELP AND RESPOND TO JACKSON

Based on my observation and insights from Melody, I also feel that Jackson's biting is related primarily to excitement/agitation that occurs when his stimulation is heightened. We saw this in the observation when his excitement with the crayons and the pegboard heightened to the point where he bit the pegboard. We often see the phenomenon of opposites at work during the toddler phase—they want to be independent and do things themselves, and they also want to have the comfort and security of their mom, dad, or caregiver. In this instance, I think we're seeing such opposites when Jackson is struggling with stimulation and strong feelings and then wanting the comfort of a trusted adult. We see this struggle when he puts himself in positions to help himself either stay calm or recover—sitting in Tasha's lap, not participating in a game that would require him to jump, seeking Kim out to pick him up and hold him while he recovered from strong feelings, seeking out the calm activity of coloring at the coloring table. At the same time, we see him enjoying activities that evoke strong feelings—even positive ones. Examples include trying to put the crayons in the pegboard, which he did with me, and happily "roaring" at other children. This may also apply to his interactions with Eddie that Melody and Tasha mentioned.

The teachers are doing so well responding to him when he needs outside help staying in control or regaining control. They should continue exactly what they are doing. We can also capitalize on one of Jackson's strengths: he shows a great deal of interest in and ability to focus on fine-motor activities. Continue to give him time with open-ended small-motor activities, such as the coloring table with the large sheets of paper. I suggest that the program put a few more small-motor materials in the room—close-ended materials, such as jumbo beads and string for stringing, shape balls, busy boards—to give Jackson even more activities he is really good at. This would give him enough stimulation to help him learn. At the same time, using these materials that he is confident and comfortable with would also help avoid overexcitement, overstimulation, and loss of control.

This is more difficult but would be very helpful. When Jackson is with a child or children who seem to heighten his stimulation, either have a teacher sit between them, or involve them in a relaxing sensory activity, such as a water table, or redirect either Jackson or the other child to another activity.

Another thing to capitalize on is Jackson's very careful observation and imitation of others. Teachers can help him figure out how to use language to avoid being overstimulated. It will help Jackson to see and hear teachers using gestures and very simple language, such as gestures that indicate *wait* or *stop* and simple words such as *oops* or *uh oh*, which indicate that something is not quite right but that are not likely to increase the level of strong feelings. If they hear him use "oops" or "uh oh," they should try to get to him as soon as possible and let him know that he said the right thing. Then they can help him with the situation that caused the comment.

Melody made the observation that teething may be a factor in the biting. I observed him putting a variety of items in his mouth and gnawing on them during the course of the hour and a half. Both of these lead me to think that oral-motor development may also play a role in his biting. Oral-motor development also plays a role in a child's learning to speak. Suggestions for this are on pages 36–37 of *No Biting*. We'll go over these together now and use them in our plan. Some of these can be done at home, which is great for Jackson's parents, who have asked their director what they could do at home to help him stop biting.

His receptive language seems to be fine; he understood everything anyone said to or around him during the observation. He used expressive language mostly in terms of gestures and movement. He used very few words and only one two-word sentence during the observation, but all were intelligible to me, a stranger. (This is a good sign!) The oral-motor activities and materials will likely enhance this budding part of his development. Specific language development suggestions for this are on pages 39–40 of *No Biting*. We'll review them together now and use them in our plan. All of these can also be done at home, which again can help Jackson's parents. Because Melody also commented on his lack of verbal language, I suggest we make a plan with the director to follow up on this with teachers and his parents. If necessary, we can request an informal language observation from the quality rating system (QRS) agency in our county.

Finally, when he does bite, we can capitalize on his strong and positive relationship with his teachers. Teachers can express disapproval of biting without being threatening or mean. Because he so obviously likes and turns to his teachers, this disapproval will send him a strong signal that biting is not all right. Suggestions for responding to Jackson when he does bite are found on pages 22–26 in *No Biting*. We'll go over them together. His teachers can follow these statements with genuine and warm offers to help him.

Observations and Suggestions for a Classroom

Sometimes we might combine both the information from teachers' observations and ours along with our suggestions to address the biting. Here is an example from an observation in a classroom in which several children had been biting:

SUGGESTIONS FOR THE RAINBOW ROOM

Observation in Classroom on March 6, 2017   8:55 a.m.–10:15 a.m.

Adults: teachers Liz and Grace

Class: nine children until 9:20 when a tenth child arrived   Observer: Gretchen Kinnell

Initial conversation with teachers on March 7

Follow-up conversation with teachers on March 8

. . . .

Several boys in the room have been biting; Ryan has been biting the most and for the longest time. He was identified as the child the teachers are most concerned about. The suggestions here are based on the classroom observation and information from the teachers.

I have four main suggestions. They involve the following:

1. Provide support and information for Ryan's parents to improve his sleep.

2. Arrange for increased staffing in the room during the time frames that the teachers say are most difficult.

3. Offer increased support for Ryan by providing more opportunities for him to be by himself or in much smaller groups doing quiet activities, and offer support in calming down.

4. Facilitate an increased level of calm in the room through changes in the types and formats of activities.

What follows are details for each of the four suggestions. These details include specific activities and practices that relate directly to what is going on in the classroom. They often include explanations about why the activities or practices would be beneficial and how to put them into place. Teachers can see how the suggestions are appropriate for toddlers, related to biting, and doable for them. These kinds of details are essential in the consulting process because they help teachers take positive action to address biting.

SUPPORT AND INFORMATION FOR RYAN'S PARENTS TO IMPROVE HIS SLEEP

One of the first things the teachers mentioned was that they felt Ryan was under a great deal of stress. They said they see it in the morning when he first arrives. His parents report that he is not sleeping well, and they also feel stressed because of this. The teachers also notice that Ryan expresses anxiety related to fears, such as seeing a visiting dental health worker dressed in a dinosaur costume. They wondered if such fears and anxiety may play a role in his sleep problems. Jackie, the center director, will contact Ryan's parents to see if they would like to meet with me to talk about ways to address these sleep issues. It sounds like working on this aspect of Ryan's life would make a big difference in his stress level and his behavior in the room.

INCREASED STAFFING IN THE ROOM

In this group, there are several children who have intense reactions in social situations. This is one of the inborn traits of temperament and is not negative, but it can be difficult when children don't yet have the skills to regulate their own behaviors. At this age, children are just learning self-control, and when they are upset, situations can escalate quite quickly. I saw this often when I observed, and Liz and Grace mentioned it as well. More adults to help interact with children would be very helpful for this. There was a noticeable difference in the group when the music teacher was in the room along with the teachers. (I also want to note that the music activity was very appropriate for this group of children. That also contributed to the calm atmosphere during the activity.) The teachers identified one time when they definitely need a third person in the room—at the beginning of the day as children are just arriving. I also noticed that during the toileting process it would be helpful to have a third person with the group. The director is willing to consider additional staffing in this room for a specified period of time. I suggest that the teachers and the director talk together to determine when a third person would be most helpful in the room. Ideally, it could be the same person for continuity.

INCREASED SUPPORT FOR RYAN

When Liz, Grace, and I met to talk about their insights and observations, the first thing they mentioned was their worry about the stress they feel Ryan is experiencing. They talked about his sleeping problems and noted that he often "arrives under stress." This sets him up for the rest of the day, and the teachers then feel under stress to figure out how to help him. They noted that he expresses many fears. For example, he was very worried during a fire drill that firefighters would arrive, and said he was scared of them. As noted before, he was also worried about the visitor dressed up as a dinosaur. Liz said, "I think he is sensitive." She has cared for Ryan since he was in the infant room and feels that he has always been sensitive like she sees with his worries. They also mentioned events in his life that are often associated with stress at this age. The family will have a new baby in three months, and in preparation for the new baby he has had to start sleeping in his own bed. His biting may well be related to the stress he feels. Liz and Grace noted that he had stopped biting about three months ago and then started again.

All of these insights cause me to think that there may be three temperament traits at work here—rhythmicity, intensity of reaction, and approach-withdrawal. Temperament is a person's preferred way of interacting with their environment, and it seems to remain constant over time. It's not destiny, and we can all learn to modify our behavior, but in times of stress most of us revert to our preferred way of interacting with the environment. There are nine temperament traits, and we look at each as a continuum. While no temperament traits are bad or negative, the ends of each continuum can make interacting with people and situations around them more difficult (or more difficult for others!). I suggest that we all work together—teachers, director, and parents—to create a temperament profile and to see how this may be contributing to the stress Ryan experiences. Having the temperament profile would help us understand Ryan better and would also help us develop effective interactions with him and activities for him. I could take the lead on this if we decide it's something we'd like to do.

Liz, Grace, and I talked about activities Ryan enjoyed and sought out, and things that seemed to help him calm down. They said that he seeks quieter activities and especially likes reading books. They mentioned that he enjoys longer books, ones that would require a longer attention period. Grace noted that reading one-on-one is especially effective at calming him. She suggested reading more with him one-on-one or in a very small group. That is an excellent suggestion and one that I think the teachers can implement easily. This could work especially well when the third adult is in the room. I would add to this suggestion that if and when the teachers notice Ryan begin to become overwhelmed, they help him by taking or directing him to this one-on-one or small-group reading. I believe the teachers have a pretty good sense of when things are—or could be—starting to become difficult for him. Intervening before he becomes overwhelmed would help him stay calm. Another suggestion is to make sure there is always a soft reading area in the room that is away from active play and to bring Ryan to that area and get him set up with a few favorite books even when teachers may not be able to read to him at that time. Being able to get away from the crowd once in a while would be helpful to him. I noticed that it was difficult for him when other children came too close to him in the room. Both teachers commented that he reacts strongly and "falls apart" when other children come close. This is not unusual for children this age because they cannot correctly gauge space. They often think people and things are closer (or farther away) than they are. If Ryan is already under stress, feeling that someone is too close to him could overwhelm him.

The teachers also mentioned that all the children including Ryan love physical attention from them; Liz pointed out that they like to get hugs from the teachers and often seek her out. Grace also talked about how much the children loved it when she massaged their arms. These are all soothing touches, and it would almost certainly help Ryan to have lots of these. Grace and I talked about the possibility of having massage be available as an activity for any child who wanted to get an arm massage. We talked about having a space where Grace would be based and even a little sign that said "massage." Children who wanted a massage could sign up using a name tag or picture card on the massage sign. This helps with name recognition and also would enable Grace to show children the list of those who wanted a massage and when each child's turn would be. This is a great cognitive activity, and the concrete list helps children begin to understand and cope with waiting and taking turns. Grace can say during every massage (for example), "John is having his massage, and then the next person will be Ryan." When children ask about their own massage, she can help them find their name on the list and where they are in the order.

Another way to support Ryan and the other children who have bitten recently (and which is also good for all the children) is to increase the amount of sensory play. To avoid overcrowding at the sensory table, teachers can have two tables open at the same time. The two tables should be in different areas of the room, and one teacher should sit with the children at each of the tables. It would be important for a teacher to sit as near Ryan as possible as support and to help him handle situations that might be difficult for him. I saw a teacher, Ana, in the Butterfly Room, do this very well with a little boy who needed this kind of support. She used a very soft voice to explain what was happening. "John is playing with the scoop now," she said when her little boy tried to take the scoop away from John. Then she used a gentle physical redirection to move the scoop back to John and said to her little boy, "Let's see how this scoop [one that was in the rice table] works," as she put it into his hands. This approach dealt with the situation at hand and did not dwell on his behavior. It kept the little boy from becoming overwhelmed and helped him return to his play easily. Ana could be a resource for Liz and Grace if they feel they'd like this kind of help and advice.

Teachers can also support Ryan by building on one of his strengths they identified. They said that he is very aware of the rules and wants them to be followed. This is a strength. Like most children this age, Ryan interprets this to mean the rules should be applied to others but not necessarily to him. Don't worry; he'll get there. But right now, teachers can help Ryan remind himself of the rules. They can ask him about a rule at a time when nothing is happening that breaks the rule. The teachers can ask him to tell them a rule and reinforce him when he does so. This helps him hear himself saying the rule and becomes a kind of self-talk, which children eventually use to remind themselves what to do. This is one way to support Ryan's own development of self-control. And it can be done at any time, except when he is upset. Let him calm down (see the activity in the next paragraph), and then use it. Even better, use it when nothing is happening—just as a kind of rule check.

Finally, teachers can help him and all the children in the room begin to learn to calm themselves down. This technique is designed to help them learn to do deep breathing, which relieves stress. It is called "Smell the Flower; Blow out the Candle." It works best if you can have a small poster with a picture or drawing of a flower and another one with a picture or drawing of a lit candle. This can be introduced as a game in which you tell the children to pretend to smell the flower as you show them the picture of the flower. Do this with them by taking a deep breath as you all "smell the flower." Then show them the picture of the candle and tell them to pretend to blow out the candle. Blow out the air slowly. This is the basic deep-breathing process made much easier for toddlers by using the ideas of a flower and a candle. You can teach this to children as a game, and then when individual children are upset, you can prompt them to "smell the flower" . . . and "blow out the candle" as you do the breathing with them. This deep breathing helps children regain control of their emotions before you try to talk with them about the situation and their behavior. The reason this is so important is that humans' brains process emotions first and thoughts second. It is literally wasting our time to try to reason with someone who is upset. Their brain simply cannot attend to the reasoning. It is too busy processing the emotion of being upset. And toddlers cannot yet do this on their own, so they need our help. This is an ideal technique for all the children—and for the adults as well!

INCREASED LEVEL OF CALM IN THE CLASSROOM

The more calm we can create, the less stress children and teachers will experience. I suggest increasing activities and formats that are calming and reducing formats that are not. One format that is very difficult for toddlers is having all of the children do the same activity at the same time. This causes children to crowd together and get too close to each other, and then end up bickering and hurting each other.

We saw this on the day I observed when Liz tried to have all the children sit down to paint. It was during this activity that we saw the most hitting, scratching, and one near bite. Liz was working so hard to get smocks on all the children; she couldn't get paper on the table for each child and also get the paints out. While she tried to get everything in place, the children were waiting, which is something toddlers simply do not do well. Painting is a wonderful activity; we don't want to avoid it but rather figure out how to do it in a way that would work more smoothly and not result in conflict. One suggestion is to use the same format described above in the massage activity. Children can come to paint a few at a time while the other children are reading with another teacher or playing in a sensory table in another area. I would also suggest that children use the easels because it is much easier for them to paint standing up than sitting down. I also suggest using smocks or shirts the children can put on themselves and taking the time to teach children to put them on and take them off. This enables children to learn an important self-help skill, cuts down on the time teachers would spend helping them, and reduces the waiting time. This also extends the activity. Painting would now involve getting your own smock, putting it on, painting, taking off the smock, and then washing your hands. You might also want to consider not using smocks at all. Many programs do this. Check that out with your director. Giving children the opportunity to paint or not to paint also helps build their sense of autonomy, which is one of the main developmental tasks of toddlers. They like knowing that they can make some decisions for themselves. It is often difficult for us as teachers to accept that not every child will choose to do an activity we set up. It's all right. At this age, it's more important that we make materials available and support children as they choose them. One of the best pieces of advice I have heard on this is that when it comes to activities for young children, "Always invite, never insist."

A format that works well for this age involves having teachers in different parts of the room actively supervising children so that they're not all crowded together in one part of the room. Children this age tend to clump around interesting adults. In this instance, *interesting* means adults who interact with the children. So if the two of you are in different parts of the room and there are interesting things to do where you are, the children will make two clumps rather than just one.

Another way to make the classroom a calmer place is to spend more time outside. I realize that as I write this, we have twenty-four inches of snow on the ground, but it will soon melt and we'll be able to go outside again. We have seen over and over that there is much less biting outdoors than indoors. There is something about being in nature and being in a larger space that is soothing. This doesn't seem to be as true as spending time in larger indoor spaces. There is something about being outdoors that is very beneficial. I suggest that you spend as much time outdoors as possible with this group. In one program the teachers actually took the children outside an additional time each day, and they saw a dramatic drop in biting when the children were inside as well as out.

In the previous section, I suggested increasing the sensory play. This is another way to make the room calmer. Water play is especially soothing to children this age, and both teachers mentioned that the children love it. Grace talked about the end of the day when she noticed that children especially started having difficulty. We talked about having small basins of water with a little soap for bubbles and letting the children who are still there wash classroom items like the dishes and plastic food from the housekeeping area. They can use sponges, scrub brushes, and dishcloths to wash these items. They can put the clean items in a large colander, which they can then help run under clear water to rinse and then lay them out to dry. You can set this up and help children learn—with lots of reminders—that they can keep washing the items while you talk with parents who come to pick up their children.

The most challenging aspect of a report like this with lots of suggestions is to choose one or two things to try, figure out how to do them, and then give it a try. It would be too stressful to try to do everything right away. My final suggestion is that teachers work with the director to let her know what suggestions they decide to try—and what help they may need. For example, it may be helpful to have someone come in to help you set up the painting activity in the way it is described here. Making a decision to try something and then giving it a good shot will help you take positive action, and that often helps reduce stress!

Here are questions to help you reflect and build skills related to developing and presenting plans and suggestions. Use either or both reports to respond to the questions below:

- ▶ In what ways do you feel the contributions of the teachers were part of these reports?

- ▶ How did the suggestions and plans match the observations and the reasons for biting?

- ▶ How useful do you feel the plans and suggestions would be to the teachers? What led you to your conclusion?

- ▶ What do you feel are the strengths of each of these plans?

- ▶ What might you want to add to the plans? What led you to consider those additions?

Developing Follow-Up Plans

After conferring with teachers, parents, and/or the director, move the conversation to what will come next:

Of all the suggestions we've talked about here, which ones might work well for you?

Of everything we've discussed, what do you think would be most important to work on first?

Help teachers, parents, or the director decide on a course of action. Listen to them and help them identify what they would like to do, how they might prioritize action steps, and how they will tackle this work. Some people like to do what is easiest for them first so they can feel a sense of accomplishment and progress. Some people like to work on small changes first; others want to dig right in and tackle big tasks first. Some people like to work on one thing at a time; others like to work on several changes at the same time. Help them clarify what would work well for them. This is the best way to keep them engaged in the process. Write down the decisions they make, and then go on to look at how to implement their plan. Use these questions to guide this discussion:

- ▶ "Who will do the various tasks in our plan?"

- ▶ "What resources or help will we need?"

- ▶ "How long do we think it will take to do the various parts of our plan?"

- ▶ "How will we decide whether it's working?"

- ▶ "If it's not working, how will we proceed?"

Here is the initial plan for the Rainbow Room:

- ▶ The teachers do want to try to get additional staffing at the beginning of the day. The director has to make that decision. They followed up with the director and got an additional person to come into the room at the beginning of the day.

- ▶ They wanted to change the way they did painting based on the report. They also wanted to take the director's suggestion and have Ana from the Butterfly Room come in and show them how to organize painting so the children could decide whether to paint and could do more of the process themselves. The director worked to make the necessary arrangements, and this was done over the course of a few weeks.

▶ They did decide they wanted to stop doing activities as one large group. They needed help to figure out how this would work. Again, they asked the director for help. She provided technical assistance in the classroom, and they made the transition over the course of a few weeks.

▶ They wanted to offer the parents an opportunity to meet with me as the consultant. The parents agreed and sent me their concerns and observations before our meeting. We framed our meeting around a temperament profile.

Here are questions to help you reflect and build skills related to developing and presenting plans and suggestions:

▶ "In what ways do you see the teachers being engaged in the planning and follow-up processes?"

▶ "How do you feel about the teachers' requests for help? What do you think it might indicate, and why does it matter?"

▶ "The plan of action here came from the teachers and the director themselves rather than from me. What do you think working in this way would be like for you? Why do you think this?"

The Last Word on the Consulting Process

The last word on the consulting process is actually a question: "Does it work?" That is, can and do programs put suggestions into practice? Does the biting stop? Do things get better? The final word on this needs to come from the people who have actually done it and have seen results. Here are the words of the director of the Rainbow Room's center: "After your consultation, we sent out a letter from one of the templates from your book to all of the parents. It seemed to help them understand more of why the children were biting and to truly trust that we were doing our best to prevent it and redirect them. The teachers took your suggestions and implemented them by adding the third teacher, including more anchoring of the children's play, and splitting up the group as often as possible. The teachers also changed the daily schedule to include more outside or gym time earlier in the day as well as a second, crunchy snack to give the children more of that input. Once the teachers and children got into the groove of the new schedule and different approach, the biting reduced significantly. We saw the children engaging in much more productive play in the classroom and more cooperative play with each other."

APPENDIX A

Sample Letters for Parents and Policy Statements for Staff and Parents

Letter Informing Parents of Plans to Address Ongoing Biting

Dear Parents,

As you know, we have been struggling with biting in our toddler room. We are all worried about it, and we know you are frustrated by it. When biting becomes an ongoing problem, our policy is to develop a plan to address it based on observation of the children and our program. We have just completed our plan and want to share it with you.

First, we noticed that most of the biting was taking place when children were crowded in the block area. Second, we noticed that the biting usually started when a child bit out of frustration, and other children responded by biting. Third, when we checked our program, we had to admit that we were not providing many sensory activities, which usually serve to calm and soothe children. Fourth, we noticed there were never any biting incidents when we went outside.

We used these observations to develop the following plan:

▶ We have made two block areas in the room so children will not be bunched up in one block area. These areas are on opposite ends of the room. We're not sure we'll keep it this way, but we want to try it for now.

▶ We are stepping up our language development activities with children who are still learning to use words to express their frustration.

▶ We have added some sensory activities and materials to the program. We have set up water play in little basins on the table. We have also added some squares of velour material (Thank you, Mrs. Jackson, for this donation) to our dress-up area.

▶ We are going to go outside one more time per day to increase the amount of time when there is no biting so children become used to a daily routine without biting.

We'll be trying these strategies for the next two weeks. During that time, we'll keep track of the biting to see if it decreases. Please bear with us. We know that positive actions work much better than negative ones, and we're doing our best to provide them.

We know this has not been a pleasant time for you, and we appreciate your support while we work to stop this biting. If you have any questions, please let us know.

Carmen Espinoza, Teacher
Nancy Jones, Teacher
LaTanya Roberts, Director

Letter Informing Parents of How the Program Approaches Biting

Dear Parents,

We are always upset when we experience biting in our toddler rooms. Even though we know biting is not entirely unexpected when toddlers are together in groups, we don't want any of your children to be bitten, and we want any child who bites to learn more appropriate behavior. When it comes to biting, here is what you can expect from us:

- ▶ We will put children's safety first and provide appropriate first aid as well as comfort, support, and advice to any child who is bitten.

- ▶ We will provide appropriate programming for toddlers to help prevent biting.

- ▶ We will make current information and resources on biting available to you.

- ▶ We will provide teachers with adequate knowledge and training to deal appropriately and effectively with biting.

- ▶ We will take your concerns seriously and treat them with understanding and respect.

- ▶ We will tell you what specific steps we are taking to address biting and explain the reasoning behind those steps.

- ▶ We will respond to your questions, concerns, and suggestions—even when our response to some suggestions is no.

- ▶ We will work to schedule conferences about biting with your child's teachers at a time when you can attend.

- ▶ We will keep your child's identity confidential if he or she bites. This helps avoid labeling or confrontations that will slow the process of learning not to bite.

Please don't hesitate to come to any of us with questions or concerns.
Sincerely,

Kirsten Petersen
Johnetta Carmichael
Cindy Chang

Sample Content on Biting for Parent Handbook

Along with all the other information we have given you about our toddler room, we want you to know about our response to biting. Biting is unfortunately not unexpected in toddler groups but can be very emotionally charged. Toddlers may bite for many reasons. Sometimes the biting is related to teething. Sometimes toddlers bite to express feelings they can't yet express with words. We have seen children bite when they are frustrated, and we have seen them bite in the excitement of a happy moment. No one can predict which children will bite, but we are ready to help toddlers who do bite learn other behavior. We are also ready to give treatment, sympathy, and advice to children who are bitten. Here are the ways we work to prevent biting and how we respond to it when it does happen.

First, we try to program the day to avoid boredom, frustration, or overstimulation. We provide a calm and cheerful atmosphere with a mix of stimulating, soothing, age-appropriate activities and multiples of favorite toys. We also work to model acceptable and appropriate behaviors for the children, helping them learn words to express their feelings and giving them tools to resolve conflicts with our help.

Second, if a bite does occur, we help the child who was bitten. We reassure him or her and care for the bite. If the skin is not broken, we use a cold pack. If the skin is broken, we follow medical advice and clean the bite with soap and water. If it is likely the bite may get dirty, we will cover it to keep it clean. If your child is bitten, we will call you to let you know about the bite. The teachers will fill out an incident report, have it signed by our administrators, keep a copy, and give one to you when you pick up your child. We also respond to the child who did the biting. We show the children strong disapproval of biting. Our specific response varies by circumstances, but our basic message is that biting is the wrong thing to do. We also help the child who bit learn different, more appropriate behavior, and we let his or her parents know there's a problem so we can work together to solve it.

Third, the teachers and administration analyze the cause of ongoing biting. We develop a plan to address the causes of the biting, focusing on keeping children safe and helping those who are stuck in biting patterns. When we need to develop such a plan, we share the details with parents so they know specifically how we are addressing this problem.

Fourth, parents are notified if their child starts to bite. We ask parents to keep us informed if their child is biting at home. Children who bite in our program do not necessarily bite at home. But if your child is biting in both places, it is important for all of us to be consistent in dealing with it. Communication is very important in order to help your child stop biting.

We wish we could guarantee that biting will never happen in our program, but we know there is no such guarantee. You can count on us to deal appropriately with biting so it will end as quickly as possible. We will support your children whether they bite or are bitten. We want the best for all the children in our program. If you want more information on biting or have any questions or concerns, please let us know.

Biting Policy

Our program recognizes that biting is unfortunately not unexpected when toddlers are in group care. We are always upset when children are bitten in our program, and we recognize how upsetting biting is for parents. While we feel that biting is never the right thing for toddlers to do, we know that they bite for a variety of reasons. Most of these reasons are not related to behavior problems. Our program does not focus on punishment for biting but on effective techniques that address the specific reason for the biting. When biting occurs, these are our three main responses:

▸ Care and help for the child who was bitten.

▸ Help for the child who bit so that he or she learns other behavior.

▸ Examination of our program to stop the biting.

Our teachers express strong disapproval of biting. They work to keep children safe and to help the child who bit learn different, more appropriate behavior. When there are episodes of ongoing biting, we develop a plan of specific strategies, techniques, and timelines to address it. We do not use any response that harms a child or is known to be ineffective.

We give immediate attention and, if necessary, first aid to children who are bitten. We offer to put ice on the bite if the child is willing. If the skin is broken, we clean the wound with soap and water. If children are bitten on the top of their hands and the skin is broken, we recommend they be seen by their health care provider.

When children bite, their parents are informed personally and privately the same day. When children are bitten, their parents are informed personally and given a copy of our incident form. When we experience ongoing biting in a toddler room, we share the written plan we have developed with all parents of children in the room.

Biting is always documented on our standard incident report form, which is completed and signed by a teacher and an administrator. It must also be signed by the parent. One copy is given to the parents, and the other copy is kept in the incident report book in the office.

We keep the name of the child who bit confidential. This is to avoid labeling and to give our teachers the opportunity to use their time and energy to work on stopping the biting.

Once a year, toddler caregivers attend a training session on biting. In addition, we have current resources on biting available for staff and parents. We encourage parents to bring their concerns and frustrations directly to the teachers.

APPENDIX B

Sample Observations

Two examples of the kinds of observations that are useful to help us craft effective plans for reducing biting are included here. These are adaptations of actual observations and the resulting recommendations. I observed the children during the course of working with teachers and used staff observations, reflections, and insights to understand the children and the settings. The resulting recommendations do not call for additional staff or for teachers to drastically alter what they do in their programs. All the recommendations can be accomplished by caring teachers in busy toddler programs.

The names of the children, the teachers, the rooms, and the centers have been changed. The observations and recommendations were made available to parents as well as teachers.

Jeffrey P., age twenty-six months, the Rainbow Room

LMNOP Child Care Center

Gretchen Kinnell, Director of Education and Training, Child Care Solutions

I had visited the Rainbow Room earlier in the month, but I came to observe Jeffrey on September 28. The observation lasted from 8:30 to 10:05 a.m. There were nine children present, ranging from twenty-four months to thirty-two months. Melissa, the head teacher, was in the room the entire time. Annie, the assistant teacher, arrived at 9:00. From 8:30 to 9:00 there was another staff person in the room who left when Annie arrived. During the time I was there, the children engaged in free play, had snack, and prepared to go outdoors.

On this visit, I noticed that the teachers were more directly involved with the children, spending more time with them one-on-one and in small groups. (During the earlier observation, the teachers were more involved with tasks in the room.) The teachers were responsive to the children as individuals and geared their interactions to the personalities and needs of each child. They also showed a genuine appreciation of and delight in each child. All the children were actively and happily engaged in activities, and there were few conflicts. This level of responsiveness and interaction will be essential in working with Jeffrey to stop the biting.

During free play, Jeffrey was very focused on his own activities. The teachers and children genuinely like him and were willing to interact with him, but he acknowledged and warmed up to other people slowly. Jeffrey played quietly by himself during most of the first forty-five minutes I observed. Although he did not play with other children (typical of toddler play), he was in close proximity to them, and none of them moved away from or avoided him. He was very focused on the toys he was playing with and at first barely acknowledged Melissa when she talked to him. He averted his gaze and kept playing with his toys. He did the same thing when another little boy came over and said, "Hi." At one point Jeffrey got his hand stuck in a toy. He cried softly, and Melissa came over to help him. He recovered very quickly.

As the morning progressed, Jeffrey began to interact more with Melissa. He sat in her lap and was quite relaxed as he smiled and listened to her. He also looked at what other children were doing and occasionally walked over near them. At 9:15, after a relaxed and uneventful period of free play, Jeffrey went to a little girl who had another train he wanted. He tried to take it from her with no words and no warning. She protested very loudly and held on to it tightly. He responded by trying to hit her and by crying loudly. His crying and attempts to hit her increased. At that point, his teacher and I both went up to him. I was the first person to reach him; I took him in my arms, rubbed his back, and used a quiet, soothing tone of voice to say, "It's so hard when you can't have what you want. I know. It's hard." He calmed down very quickly and then was easily redirected by his teacher to something else. At 9:25 there was another incident that was almost identical. It was a different child and a different toy, but Jeffrey quickly began to cry and tried to hit. His teacher handled the situation much the same way I had in the earlier incident. At 9:28 there was a third incident that was again identical to the first two. Melissa said that this was typical of the situations that had led to his biting in the past.

Immediately after the 9:28 incident, it was time for snack. Jeffrey was the first person to seat himself at the table. He buckled himself in and played with a toy by himself quite contentedly until the rest of the children were seated. He did not interact with the other children during snack. He yawned and had second helpings, and he was the last child to leave the snack table—by his own choice. We know that toddlers often bite when they are physically tired, hungry, or overwhelmed. Perhaps snacktime was an opportunity for Jeffrey to regroup.

From observing Jeffrey and talking with Melissa, several patterns emerged that will form the basis for the plan to help him learn to stop biting. First was that when Jeffrey played by himself, he did quite well, but when he initiated contact with other children, it was often to get something he wanted. He didn't use language but just tried to take the object.

Second, he wasn't able to manage his emotional response to the situation when he met resistance. I want to note that this is in no way a deficiency; it is quite typical of toddlers. Left on his own, he became more and more emotionally distraught. However, he responded very positively and very quickly to being comforted and soothed by an adult. This is a very good sign because self-control develops from external to internal. He responded very well to external help and did not fight it. It was also evident from the timeline of the incidents that once he began to have trouble dealing with his emotions, it escalated. In the last incident, the little girl decided to give Jeffrey the toy. The teachers said this little girl is quite aware of other children's feelings, and she gave him the toy willingly. He accepted the toy, played with it for a minute or so, and then gave it back to her and said, "Thank you." He knows what to do, and when he is not emotionally bound up, he can do it. But when he is struggling with strong emotions, he cannot regain control by himself.

Third, from the toys he selected and the way he played with them, it was evident that Jeffrey has very good small-motor skills for his age. He was very focused in his small-motor play. He is one of the youngest children in the room, but he hitched the cars of a toy train together and could easily buckle the little seat belts on the chairs. Two other children tried to hitch the train cars but could not do it. They could see how the cars should go together but did not have the fine-motor skills to do it. Melissa reported that of the ten children in the room, only three can fasten the seat belts, and Jeffrey is one of them. Jeffrey was also very persistent when working on various tasks with toys. He put a helmet on and spent two minutes turning and turning it until it fit just right.

It is possible that Jeffrey's persistence may play a role in his biting. Melissa said that even though Jeffrey often bit when he had conflicts with other children over toys, he sometimes bit after the conflict was over. He would walk away seemingly composed and then bite someone else, sometimes even later. It seems that Jeffrey also may be persistent in his need to express his frustration.

Plan to Help Reduce Jeffrey's Biting

First, the teachers should continue giving Jeffrey the positive attention and gentle physical interactions he enjoys. They should continue to support his play when he is playing alone and at the same time point out what other children around him are doing. This will help him become more aware of others. Second, even more effective than having one person shadowing him is having the teachers who interact with him most watch for situations in which he may not be able to manage his emotions. When that happens, the first step should be to move in, move him away from the other child (or move the other child away from him), and help him calm down with circular motions or gentle pats on the back, a soothing tone of voice, and words that acknowledge how hard it is for him. When he does calm down, he needs to be told that the other child is playing with the toy now and that he can play with something else. This should be followed by redirecting him to a different toy and by reinforcing his calming down with a short comment like "Good for you. Now you're fine and playing with a ball." The teachers did a very good job of this on the day I observed. They knew exactly what kind of toy to redirect him to. This approach will provide the external control he needs at this point, which will be the foundation on which he can develop internal control.

The teachers should also help Jeffrey learn new social skills by watching for times when he wants a toy another child has. If they can intervene before he begins getting upset, they can tell him, "You're looking at the train. Jackie has it now. Ask Jackie, 'Please?' Maybe you can play with it." Then, of course, give Jackie the option of saying yes or no. If she says no, the teachers should say matter-of-factly, "Jackie still wants to play with it." Redirect Jeffrey to something else. Little by little, the teachers can help him learn more and more of the language of asking for something. He has already shown that he is able to apply this kind of social skill when he is not emotionally embroiled.

The teachers can also help Jeffrey develop competence at interacting with other children by playing with him for a minute or so with a toy designed to go back and forth between two people, like a ball. Then the teacher can invite another child to come over and play too. The teachers should choose a child who is likely to agree to do this. The teacher should then stay close to Jeffrey to support him as he plays with the other child. This does not have to last long. It will give Jeffrey some supported and successful interactions with other children.

We also want to capitalize on Jeffrey's interest, fine-motor skills, and persistence. He has already mastered the fine-motor toys in the room. Let's try bringing in toys from other classrooms that require more advanced fine-motor skills. At first you'll probably need to bring in duplicates of the toys because, being new, the toys will interest other children and they will want to explore them too. This will give Jeffrey the opportunity to feel the satisfaction that comes with doing something he enjoys and is good at.

Finally, the teachers must be aware of Jeffrey's physical needs. He had more trouble managing his emotions when he was hungry and tired and after he had already had other emotional episodes. He recovered after having his snack and having time when he did not interact with other children. Teachers might schedule short one-on-one lap times with Jeffrey at around 9:15—just before snack—to give him the physical support that seems to help him emotionally. Teachers should also point out to him when he has used language to thank someone for sharing or to ask for something. This will be his clue that these are the behaviors to continue.

Matthew R., age twenty-one months, the Sunshine Room

XYZ Child Care Center

Gretchen Kinnell, Director of Education and Training, Child Care Solutions

I observed Matthew in his classroom on October 26 from 9:00 to 10:30 a.m. There were four children in the room during the observation, ages seventeen months through twenty-five months. Amber, the teacher, was there the entire time. Candace, another teacher, arrived at 9:10 and was there for the remainder of the time. While I was there, the children engaged in free play, had snack, and played in the gross-motor room. The teachers also changed diapers as necessary.

I observed four types of behavior that I think relate to Matthew's biting and will be keys to developing an approach to help him learn to stop biting.

First, he has a great deal of oral-motor activity—he puts everything in his mouth. He also enjoys manipulating his mouth to make sounds. During the observation, he

> ▶ sucked his thumb while Candace read to him;

> ▶ put a puppet's big plastic eyes in his mouth so that the rest of the puppet was hanging out of his mouth;

> ▶ specifically sought the smaller balls in the gross-motor area so that he could get his mouth on them more easily;

> ▶ put small toys—cars and a toy ambulance—in his mouth;

> ▶ made "raspberry" sounds and seemed quite delighted with himself;

> ▶ exchanged a big, round ball for a football after he couldn't get his mouth on the round ball very well. As soon as he had the football, he put the end in his mouth and smiled;

> ▶ sought out and enthusiastically used musical instruments that work by blowing into them;

> ▶ kept a small ball in his mouth even when trying to climb up a step in the gross-motor room; and

> ▶ had his mouth wide open much of the time, whether he was smiling broadly or crying.

Second, I observed that Matthew sought out contact with other adults and children. He readily ran up to me when I came into the room, even though he had never seen me before. He enjoyed physical attention with his teachers, sitting in Candace's lap as she read him a book, and hugging both Candace and Amber often. As is typical of toddlers, Matthew played near other children but not with them.

He handed them toys and kept one eye on what they were doing. On one occasion, he hit Liam when Liam got too close to him. Candace and Amber often redirected children—including Matthew—when they got very close together and began to tussle over toys.

Third, I observed that Matthew had rapidly developing language abilities and he delighted in his own speech. During my stay, he pointed at toys and, making sure I was paying attention, announced, "Ball!" "Kitty!" "Dog!" He was very engrossed in a story Candace read with him one-on-one. He pointed to a picture of a boy in the book and told Candace quite insistently, "Mack!" Candace then told me that Matthew has an older brother, Max, who looks a bit like the boy in the picture. At snacktime, Candace and Amber were talking with the children about their families, and Matthew pointed to Candace and then looked at me and said, "Mack bus." His speech was not completely clear, but within a very short time, Candace and I understood what he was saying. Not only was Matthew telling me (correctly, as it turned out) that Max was on the bus, but by pointing to Candace he was indicating that he knew Candace had put Max on the bus. This type of sentence, called a *telegraphic sentence* because it only includes the key words, is one of the milestones in language development for toddlers.

Finally, I saw Matthew try to get into small, semiprivate spaces several times. He tried about three times to go into the space behind the classroom door, which was open. He also climbed into the bottom shelf of the bookshelf, which was just a few inches above the floor.

Plan to Reduce Matthew's Biting

While Matthew did not bite during the morning I observed him, we can use these observations to look at why he might be biting and to formulate a plan to help him stop. First, a great deal of toddler biting is related to oral-motor exploration, and Matthew exhibited a constant need for oral-motor involvement. To help address this need and reduce the likelihood of biting, physical and occupational therapists recommend that children be allowed opportunities to explore with their mouths. Here are several suggestions:

▶ Allow him to put things in his mouth as long as they are safe. (Set aside items he has mouthed for later disinfecting. You can disinfect toys by washing and spraying them with a solution of one part bleach to ten parts water and allowing the toys to air-dry. This would be true for toys all children mouth, not just those that Matthew mouths.)

▶ Give him oral-motor activities on a daily basis—blowing bubbles is a good one.

- ▸ Have him play musical instruments that require blowing to make sound.

- ▸ Have him blow pinwheels to make them go around and around.

- ▸ Have him blow on crepe paper streamers to make them move.

- ▸ Have him blow on wind chimes to make sounds.

Second, Matthew does not know what to do with other toddlers when they get too close to him or when they do things he doesn't like. This is often a reason toddlers bite. Amber and Candace should continue watching toddlers who are interacting, notice when conflicts start to develop, and then redirect the children away from each other.

Third, they can begin putting language with situations. Many toddlers bite when they do not have language to express themselves, so I suggest capitalizing on Matthew's exploding language acquisition by engaging in conversations with him, verbally describing situations, and putting words to actions and things. An example would be, "Oh dear. Liam has the ball, and Matthew wants it. Liam is playing with it now. Let's find another ball for Matthew." This gives Matthew an explanation of what is going on and guides him toward a solution that does not involve biting (or hitting, for that matter). And the more competence he has with language, the more likely it is that he will not bite.

Finally, since Matthew sought and enjoyed being in small, private spaces, the teachers should create some. It might be a large cardboard box that has a door and is open on the top (and anchored by a pillow) so he can be by himself and still be under their supervision. They will probably have to make more than one of these, since other children will also love them.

APPENDIX C

Incident Report Forms

INCIDENT REPORT

Child's name _____ Child's age _____

Date of incident ____ /____ /____   Time of incident _____ ☐ AM ☐ PM

How was the child injured? What was the child doing when hurt?

_____

_____

_____

Were other children or adults involved? How?

_____

_____

_____

Location and description of the injury:

_____

_____

_____

Was any care given on-site? (Circle one)   YES   NO   If yes, describe:

_____

_____

_____

Was the child's parent/guardian notified? (Circle one)   YES   NO

Was a physician contacted? (Circle one)   YES   NO   By whom? _____

When? _____   Physician name: _____

Describe any advice given by physician on the back of this report.

Recommendation for future injury prevention: _____

_____

Signature of staff member _____   Date _____

Signature of additional witness _____   Date _____

Signature of parent/guardian _____   Date _____

Office Copy (Original) ☐   Parent/Guardian Copy ☐   Child's Folder Copy ☐

INCIDENT REPORT

Child's name _____ Child's age _____

Date of incident ____ /____ /____

Time of incident _____ ☐ AM ☐ PM

Type of incident _____
(accident, illness, etc.)

Place _____
(playground, name of classroom, etc.)

Describe the incident:

_____

_____

_____

Describe the injuries:

_____

_____

_____

First aid or other attention provided:

_____

_____

_____

Parent/guardian notified (Circle one)   YES   NO   Parent signature _____

Date: ____ /____ /____   Time: _____ ☐ AM ☐ PM

Signature of staff completing report _____

Signature of witness _____

INCIDENT REPORT

Child's name _____ Date ___/___/___ Time _____ ☐ AM ☐ PM

Cause and description of injury or accident:

_____

_____

_____

_____

Action taken / first aid given:

_____

_____

_____

_____

Additional comments / follow-up:

_____

_____

_____

_____

Staff signature _____ Date report completed ___/___/___

Parent/guardian signature _____ Date ___/___/___

Guide to Using the Biting Incident Documentation and Reflection Form

All bites should be documented as incident reports as mentioned on page 32. There are times when the reason for a bite may be very clear; for example, when one child grabs a toy from another. In this instance, we can document that bite and quite easily address it. Many times, however, we need additional documentation for ourselves so we can look more closely at the biting and use the information to decide how to address it. This might be when we are not sure why a child bit or when a child's biting becomes a pattern. The Biting Incident Documentation and Reflection Form that follows was created for that purpose.

"Finding out why a particular toddler is biting requires thoughtful observation." This statement from *No Biting* is at the heart of our work when toddlers bite. This form is a tool to help you record not only your observations about a specific biting incident but also the factors related to the incident. Recording this information sets the stage for the thoughtful reflection that can help you discern the reason for the biting. In some instances, you may feel the reason for the biting is quite clear. When it doesn't seem so clear, you may want to confer with colleagues, and the information you have recorded on this form will be the basis for such a discussion. Once you feel that you have a good understanding of the reason(s) for the biting, you are in a good position to decide what to do.

This guide offers tips on using this form. Clearly it requires time to complete and time is often in very short supply in busy toddler rooms. However, it is time well spent because it is so helpful in thinking more deeply about the biting and responses to it. Completing the form doesn't require an extended period of time, because the best way to do it is in two installments. The first includes the section at the top and the "Before," "During," and "After" boxes. These can be completed fairly easily. The four questions at the bottom call for analysis and reflection. Most teachers find it helpful to take some time to think these questions through before completing this part of the form. It can be completed a day or so after the incident.

USING THE FORM

Fill in the information on the first three lines. Be specific about the date and time of the biting incident; you may need to revisit this information later. Details about where the biting took place are very important. If biting occurred on the playground, be specific about exactly where on the playground the incident happened. These kinds of details become important in understanding the biting and figuring out how to address it. This is especially true when there are patterns of biting in the same place. If, for example, several forms indicate that biting happened in the sandbox, you know to focus on the sandbox. The information in the "Before" and "During" boxes on those forms (see below) can help you understand why so many bites took place in the sandbox. You might decide to take a more in-depth look at sandbox play. Use detailed questions to get a better understanding of the sandbox bites. Here are examples of such detailed questions:

▶ How many children are playing in the sandbox at any given time?

▶ Is the sandbox large enough for that many children without overcrowding?

▶ Are there enough toys in the sandbox to facilitate play?

▶ Are there multiples of favorite toys, such as sifters, dump trucks, or rubber dinosaurs?

▶ What kind of supervision are we providing in the sandbox?

BEFORE, DURING, AND AFTER

In these three boxes, write specific details you can remember about the time before the biting incident, during the incident itself, and after the incident. Ask yourself what occurred in the classroom ten to fifteen minutes before the biting took place as well as fifteen minutes after the incident. When considering what took place *during* the incident, be specific about the children involved, materials they were using, activities they were doing, the adult supervision, and any relevant developmental information.

Additional possible considerations include the following:

▶ activities that were taking place in other areas of the room

▶ group sizes

▶ language development and language used by children

▶ cues to indicate biting was likely going to happen (a child taking a toy, a child yelling "No!" to another child, a child showing changes in mood)

▶ staff reaction to the biting incident

▶ child-to-child interactions

▶ children's reaction to the biting

▶ transitions that may have been taking place in the room

▶ information parents may have shared on biting at home or other stresses at home

▶ the overall level of stimulation in the classroom

▸ the overall atmosphere of the classroom

▸ any possible disruptions in the schedule

What cues/signals, if any, did you see that a biting incident might occur?

In this section, consider anything that alerted you to the biting when, or even before, it happened. Here are examples of possible cues and signals:

▸ Were the children involved expressing frustration or anger?

▸ Did you see the child who bit chewing on toys or on their hand or blanket beforehand?

▸ Did the child bite, or attempt to bite, earlier or at home that morning?

▸ Is the child able to express feelings with words?

▸ Were too many children gathered in a small space and beginning to push each other?

▸ Did a child get too close to the child who bit?

▸ How did adult(s) respond to this bite?

Often, when we think of staff responses to biting, we automatically consider things such as these:

▸ Did staff comfort the child who was bitten?

▸ Was the bite area cleaned?

▸ Did staff speak to the child who bit to explain that we don't bite others?

▸ Was the incident documented on the proper report form?

While all of the above are important, they are probably a matter of following program procedures and wouldn't have to be included here. For this form, we want to consider the quality of the interaction(s) between the adult(s) and the child(ren). We might include

▸ whether the adult(s) responded to the child(ren) calmly;

▸ whether the adult(s) might have overwhelmed the child who bit by talking too much or giving too many directions;

▸ whether and how the adult(s) met the emotional needs of both the child who bit and the child who was bitten;

▸ whether the adult(s) offered replacement behaviors to the child who bit to give him or her alternatives to biting; and

▸ whether the adult(s) checked in later in the day with the child who bit to offer emotional support and to comment on and support appropriate behaviors.

REFLECTION

Looking at these notes, what are your thoughts about the reason(s) for the biting? Read over the information on this form carefully, keeping in mind the many reasons toddlers might bite. This information is in chapter 1. You may be surprised by how many ideas and insights your notes elicit. Write down your thoughts on the reason(s) for the biting. If you are not quite sure about your conclusions or feel it would be useful to have a second informed opinion, confer with another teacher or your director.

WHAT PRACTICES MIGHT BE EFFECTIVE TO ADDRESS THIS BITING?

Use the information in chapters 2 and 3 to decide what practices might be effective to address this biting. The practices you put in place can help you respond to this child if biting continues. They may also reduce the potential for future biting. Keep in mind that the practices can include interactions, activities, materials, language, and changes to the environment and schedule. Write down the practices you believe would be most valuable. Again, if you would like to have another opinion, share this completed form and discuss your ideas with a colleague.

BITING INCIDENT DOCUMENTATION AND REFLECTION FORM

Child's name _____   Form completed by _____

Date of biting incident ____ /____ /____   Time incident occurred _____ ☐ AM ☐ PM

Where did the incident take place?

_____

Describe what was happening in the classroom before, during, and after the biting occurred.

Before	During	After

What cues / signals, if any, did you see that a biting incident might occur?

_____

_____

How did adult(s) respond to this bite?

_____

_____

Reflection

Looking at these notes, what are your thoughts about the reason(s) for the biting?

_____

_____

What practices might be effective to address this biting?

_____

_____

Curriculum for Staff Orientation
and Training on Biting

Here is the curriculum mentioned in chapter 5 that is based on *No Biting* and can be used to orient and train staff. It is a fully developed, ready-to-use curriculum organized into eight short modules. The modules, which are designed to take about thirty to forty minutes each, can be offered individually or grouped together when longer time frames are available. Each module has a simple one-page handout.

MODULE 1 Introduction to the Biting Dilemma in Toddler Classrooms

Overview of the Module

Module 1 introduces participants to biting as a unique dilemma in toddler classrooms. It also introduces the concept that the actions we take and the responses and decisions we make about biting are based on how we think about it—that is, our perspective on it. Finally, participants will review their own program's perspective on biting.

Objectives

▶ Participants will examine what it is about biting that makes it such a difficult issue.

▶ Participants will understand the role of perspective in responding to biting.

▶ Participants will examine in depth their program's perspective on biting.

Segments

1. Introduction to the biting dilemma in toddler classrooms

2. Understanding the importance of perspective in responding to biting

3. Reviewing your own program's perspective on biting

Preparation

Make copies of the module 1 handout for everyone. Let participants know that this handout has information so they don't have to try to write down everything themselves as well as room for them to take their own notes.

SEGMENT 1

Welcome everyone. Put the overview into your own words and share it with them.
   Begin this segment with this discussion question:

. . . .

"No one likes it when toddlers hit, kick, push, or shove. But there is something about biting that just seems so much worse. Why do you think that is?"

. . . .

Participants can work in pairs first, and then you can bring the pairs together to hear everyone's responses. If the group is small, you can work as a large group. As people share their ideas, ask whether anyone else had the same or a similar idea. They can give a thumbs-up or a verbal response like "Yes" or "I agree." This gives everyone a way to participate even if their ideas were mentioned by someone else. It also indicates the level of agreement with specific ideas.

The most usual responses are variations on these themes. If they don't arise, bring them up yourself:

▸ There are so many germs. It's so dirty.

▸ It leaves a mark that looks terrible and lasts a long time.

▸ It really hurts.

▸ It's scary.

▸ It's like a violation.

▸ It's so personal.

▸ It's animalistic.

Talk more about the last two. We can hit each other from arm's length. We can kick each other from a distance of more than a foot. But to bite someone, we have to be right on top of them. Our mouths have to be right on their flesh. That's personal! We think of biting as something animals do; we generally don't associate it with people. So biting seems very primal, very animalistic, wild, out of control. That means the person who bites almost seems more like an animal than a person. And that is frightening.

Continue with this discussion question:

. . . .

"So if we can identify what makes biting so upsetting, think of a parent's reaction when his or her toddler is bitten by another child. On a scale of one to ten, how emotionally charged might biting be for parents?"

. . . .

Have participants share their rating, and ask them how they arrived at that rating. Use the discussion method of checking for agreement as outlined above.

Finally, ask participants to reflect on what biting has been like for them, or, if they have not yet experienced it, to think of what it might be like when toddlers bite in their care. Let each participant share their comments with the group.

Conclude this segment by pointing out that we've just analyzed why biting seems so much worse than other toddler behaviors and so emotionally charged for parents. We've also thought about what it has been like or what it might be like for us when toddlers bite in our care.

SEGMENT 2

This segment is based on the information in the sections "Describing Biting," "Assumptions about Biting," and "Program Perspectives on Biting" in the introduction to *No Biting*, pages 4–7. Use this content as you present this segment.

Direct participants to the handout and look together at the exchange at the top of the page:

. . . .

"Why don't you just tell me what to do about biting, and I'll do it?"

"First things first, how should we look at biting?"

"Wait! Why does it matter how we look at biting?"

. . . .

Use the material below as a short follow-up:

Most people can identify with these sentiments. Sometimes we just want the answer! We don't want the big, long explanation, and we don't want to have to do a lot of thinking. We just want to get on with it. We want to go straight to actions. But let's take a look at where our actions come from. (Direct participants to the second half of the handout.) This model shows that the things we do—our actions—come from our goals, and our goals come from our attitudes, perspectives, and beliefs. *Perspective*, of course, means how you look at something. Here is an example of this model in action from a real-life, nonbiting situation.

A middle-age woman had always ironed all her sheets, pillowcases, towels, and washcloths. She had done this week after week for over thirty years. Her younger niece repeatedly chided her about this, telling her it wasn't necessary. Finally, the woman agreed to try not doing all this ironing. The next wash day, she folded the sheets, pillowcases, towels, and washcloths without ironing them first and put them into the linen closet. The next day her husband called the niece. "Thanks a lot!" he said. "My wife tossed and turned all night, until she finally jumped out of bed at four in the morning and ironed everything."

When the niece called her aunt, the older woman said, "I just couldn't leave those things unironed. What if I died in the middle of the night? My friends would come and help my husband clean the house, and they would find those sheets, pillowcases, towels, and washcloths all wrinkled, and they would think I was not a good wife and mother."

It turns out that the aunt believes that good wives and mothers iron sheets and pillowcases, towels, and washcloths. That's her perspective; that's the way she sees it. And that leads to her goal, which is to be a good wife and mother. That then drives her to do all that ironing. Her niece had a different perspective of being a good wife and mother, but it didn't matter to her aunt. What mattered was how she saw it.

This is humorous, and it illustrates the importance of perspective. Perspectives are at the root of our actions.

Lead participants in this activity about biting perspectives. Introduce the following perspectives on biting one at a time. For each one, discuss with participants what kinds of actions that perspective would call for. Each example has some notes to help you with this.

▶ Perspective: Biting is a toddler crime!

- If biting is a toddler crime, then the goal must be to extract justice and punish the little toddler criminals. It follows that the actions you will use are all punishments. Now ask everyone to think of common punishments and how those work with toddlers (time-out, being sent to the director's office, having something foul sprayed in their mouths, and so on). Finally, consider how well these would work to stop the biting.

▶ Perspective: All biting is an indication that something is wrong at home.

- If all biting is an indication that something is wrong at home, then the goal is always and only to figure out what it is. The actions, then, all revolve around finding out what's going on at home. (Interviewing parents over and over until you discover what's wrong, trying to get it out of the child, asking other staff if they know.) Finally, consider how well these would work to stop the biting. Note that this perspective is especially inappropriate because it keeps teachers from looking for the real reason(s) the child is biting, and it destroys any chance of a positive relationship with the parents.

▶ Perspective: Biting just happens.

- If biting just happens, then the goal is just to live with it. And there would be no actions because there's nothing anyone can do about biting. Consider how well this perspective would work to stop the biting.

Direct participants to the perspective on the handout; there are seven statements in this perspective. Review each of the bullets carefully and discuss any or all of them with these questions:

. . . .

"This perspective is described as 'realistic and helpful in deciding what to do.' What is it about the perspective that makes it realistic and helpful? How would it help us decide what to do?"

. . . .

....

"We have seen that our actions flow from the way we see things—our perspective. If this is our perspective, what might our actions be? What kinds of actions would we not see if this is our perspective?"

....

You can also use this information from *No Biting* to summarize the importance of perspective:

....

"This perspective leads to two very worthwhile goals: to support toddlers whether they bite or are bitten and to support parents when biting occurs. With these goals in mind, you'll be less likely to look for the one perfect technique to implement, the one-size-fits-all plan for whenever biting occurs. Instead, as a professional, you will approach each instance of biting from a problem-solving perspective. You will take into account developmental factors, treat each toddler as a unique individual, and look critically at the role of your caregiving environment in supporting or discouraging biting. That way you'll always have alternatives, unlike the people locked into their one "perfect" technique, who inevitably find themselves not knowing what to do when it doesn't work. You will be like a master craftsperson who designs a plan for each specific situation and carefully carries out that plan."

....

SEGMENT 3

This is your opportunity to share your program's perspective on biting. Note that there is room on the handout for participants to take notes. Give everyone a copy of the program's perspective on biting. Review it carefully and thoroughly together. Then continue with any or all of the following:

- ▶ Explain how the program developed the perspective. If it is very similar to the perspective on the handout, explain why the program decided to adopt it.

- ▶ Explain how this perspective shapes what the program does when biting occurs. Be specific and, if possible, give examples from the program's own experiences.

- ▶ Ask whether and how the teachers have seen evidence of the program's perspective in practice.

- ▶ Ask participants what kinds of actions they predict would result from this perspective.

▶ Check whether the participants have questions about the program's perspective or what kinds of actions it might require from them.

Conclusion

Express your appreciation for people's participation. Let them know where they can bring any questions they may have. Let them know that more information is available in *No Biting*, and tell them where they can find the book in your program.

"Why don't you just tell me what to do about biting, and I'll do it?"

"First things first, how should we look at biting?"

"Wait! Why does it matter how we look at biting?"

Here's a perspective that is realistic and helpful in deciding what to do:

► We understand and accept that when toddlers are in groups, biting is unfortunately not unexpected.

► We know and accept that toddlers bite for many reasons.

► We believe that biting is never the right thing to do.

► We want to help children who are bitten feel better by providing comfort, care, support, and advice.

► We want children who bite to learn different, more appropriate behavior.

► We understand that our caregiving environment and practices can influence biting, and we take responsibility for ensuring they are appropriate for toddlers.

► We understand that biting is very difficult for parents, and we communicate with them thoughtfully and frankly.

Perspectives and Beliefs ➡ Goals ➡ Actions

Here is what we want you to know about our program's perspective on biting and how we use it:

MODULE 2 Why Toddlers Might Bite and Related Practices: Reasons Related to Development, Part 1

Overview of the Module

Module 2 introduces participants to the understanding that toddlers bite for a number of reasons and that our responses to biting work best when they match the reason(s) the child bit. In this module, we'll take an in-depth look at five of these reasons.

Objectives

▸ Participants will understand that toddlers bite for many reasons.

▸ Participants will understand the importance of determining the reason a specific child bites.

▸ Participants will study five reasons toddlers bite and corresponding strategies and techniques.

Segments

1. The importance of understanding reasons toddlers bite

2. The role of development in biting

3. Reasons related to developmental factors and practices to address them

- teething pain or discomfort
- oral-motor development
- sensory exploration
- experimenting with cause and effect
- imitating

Preparation

Make copies of the module 2 handout for everyone. Tell participants that this is a working handout with a chart for their own ideas and notes. Read and become familiar with chapter 1, "Why Do Toddlers Bite?" and the sections on teething, oral-motor development, sensory exploration, experimenting with cause and effect, and imitating in chapter 3 of *No Biting*.

SEGMENT 1

Welcome everyone. Put the overview into your own words and share it with them. Ask participants if the following exchange sounds familiar:

....

"Once we have a good, solid perspective in place, we realize that
if we want to be effective, we have to understand toddler biting."
"I don't want to understand it. I just want it to stop."

....

Let participants respond to that last statement. Acknowledge that most of us have surely felt that way at one time or another! We're human. We get frustrated. We just want the biting to stop. Acknowledging this allows us to put it in its place and make room for a different way of approaching biting. Here's a folktale that will help us do that. Learn it well enough to present it easily.

Once upon a time in the early 1900s, a family in Mississippi lived on a farm a few miles from a small village. Everyone in the family spent almost all their time on the farm. But the daughter who was seven years old went to school in the village every day, walking there in the morning and coming home in the late afternoon.

She was often given little jobs to complete in the village on her way home from school, mostly going to the general store. On a very hot day at the beginning of the school year, her grandma told her to stop at the general store and pick up a big chunk of butter. She was going to bake her special butter cake for the church picnic on Sunday. She said that Mrs. Smith at the store was familiar with her excellent cake and would know how much butter she needed. So the little girl said she would. After school she went to the store and told Mrs. Smith what she needed. Mrs. Smith knew exactly what she meant and came out of the ice shed with a big chunk of butter. She gave it to the little girl. The little girl put it in her pocket and began the long walk home. When she got home, her grandma asked her whether she had gotten the butter. "Yes, I did!" said the little girl proudly. She went to get it from her pocket, but the butter had melted and all she had was a big grease spot on her skirt.

Her grandmother said, "You shouldn't have put it in your pocket. What you should have done was taken it to the stream, wrapped it in some nice big leaves, and held it under the water for a good ten minutes or so, and then run home with it as fast as you could go."

The little girl replied, "Oh, now I know what to do." The next day her brother Fred asked her to stop by the general store because his friend in the village had promised to give him one of his hamsters. He said he'd leave the hamster at the general store for Fred sometime after school started. School had started, and Fred wanted his sister to check and bring the hamster home for him. She said she would be glad to do it and added, "And I know exactly what to do."

She went to the general store after school, and Mrs. Smith was there waiting with the hamster for Fred. The little girl quickly took it to the stream, wrapped it in a large leaf, and held it under the water for a good ten minutes. Then she ran home and handed Fred . . . a dead hamster.

Fred said, "You shouldn't have held it under water. You should have made a little leash and let the hamster follow you home."

The little girl replied, "Oh, now I know what to do." The next day her mother asked her to see if Mrs. Smith had any stale bread so she could make bread pudding. The little girl said she would be glad to do it and added, "And I know exactly what to do." She went to the general store after school, and Mrs. Smith did indeed have a loaf of stale bread. So the little girl tied a string around the bread and dragged it home behind her. When she got home, there was nothing but a small, filthy lump. And the path home was covered with crumbs.

Her mother said, "You shouldn't have tied a string around it and dragged it home behind you. You should have taken a paper bag with you and put it in there."

The little girl replied, "Oh, now I know what to do." The next day, her father asked her to bring home a half gallon of molasses from Mrs. Smith's store. He asked his daughter if she could carry that much molasses. "Yes," the little girl replied, "and I know exactly what to do."

This tale goes on and on, but we get the point. Discuss the point of this tale with participants, making sure that you eventually get to the idea that the best way to bring one thing home was exactly the wrong way to bring another thing home. The way we respond to a situation depends on the details of that situation. We can easily apply this to biting: the way we respond to a child who bites depends on the details of the biting. And one of the most important details in biting is the reason behind it.

SEGMENT 2

Introduce this segment with the following:

No Biting lists quite a number of reasons toddlers might bite. Those reasons are organized into three broad categories: reasons related to development, to expression of feelings, and to an environment or program that is not working for the child. In this module, we'll look at five reasons related to development. In the next module, we'll look at five more.

Remind participants of this statement from the biting perspective in module 1: "When toddlers are in groups, biting is unfortunately not unexpected." The reason it's not unexpected is because so many toddlers bite. Some people even describe biting as "a phase." This is not exactly true because biting is a behavior, but almost all biting happens in the toddler phase of development.

Here's a short activity to illustrate the point. Present it to participants like this:

Think of someone you know personally who can be very frustrating to you. It might be a friend, family member, or colleague. Please raise your hand when you have a person in mind. (Wait for participants to raise their hands.) Now think of a time when you felt very, very frustrated with that person. Keep your hand up as you think about that. Now, keep your hand up if you bit that person.

Every hand is likely to go down. Ask participants why they didn't bite the other person. Most will respond that they were mad enough to bite, but they stopped themselves; they knew it would not be right to bite. That understanding is related to our developmental level. We can get frustrated, but we can use language, we know how to take our frustration down a notch, and we know how to stop ourselves from doing something we know we should not do. These are all characteristics of the adult stage of development. Toddlers aren't in that stage; they are in the toddler stage of development. They are easily frustrated, they don't have the language to express their frustration adequately, and they can't regulate or control their own behavior very easily. This often results in biting.

SEGMENT 3

Direct participants to the chart on the handout. Some boxes are filled in and others are not. Here is how to use the chart to present, discuss, and work on the five reasons related to development.

1. Work on one reason at a time. Present the reason and the short explanation given in the box on the left. Check in with participants and ask how many of them are familiar with this.

   • "In this first box, we see teething pain and discomfort along with the explanation that children this age are often teething, and they gnaw on things for relief. Sound familiar? How many of you have had toddlers who were miserable because they were teething and may have been chewing on things?"

   • Ask participants, "How might the pain of teething result in a bite?" Give them time to respond. This is crucial to the learning process. It gives participants the opportunity to make the connection between the reason and the actual bite.

2. Next, look at the middle box, "What you might see." Ask participants to think of what they might see that would indicate that the reason for a particular bite was the pain and discomfort of teething. Ask them to write one of their ideas in the middle box, saving room for the ideas of other participants. Then ask participants to share their ideas with the group. Participants can create a list in that middle box as everyone shares their ideas. Here are some possible indicators. If all of these do not emerge from the group, add them yourself:

   • The child who bit had been chewing on lots of different toys before biting.

   • The child had bitten a toy.

   • The child had been miserable before biting, crying and rubbing his mouth.

   • The child who bit was mouthing the child he ended up biting.

   This is important because it helps participants understand that identifying the reason a toddler bites is a matter of observation.

3. Now look at the box on the right, "What you can do when this is the reason." This is the point at which we identify strategies and techniques that are directly related to the reason the child is biting, in this case the pain and discomfort from teething. Present the material directly from the section on teething in chapter 3 of *No Biting*. Encourage participants to write their own notes in the box on their handout. Ask them if they have additional ideas for that box, keeping in mind that the strategies and techniques must relate to the pain and discomfort of teething.

Repeat this format for each of the other four reasons related to development on the handout. Here are the references in *No Biting* for each of the other reasons:

   ▶ Information on oral-motor development as a reason for biting is on page 11 in chapter 1. Suggestions for strategies and techniques are on pages 36–37 in chapter 3.

   ▶ Information on sensory exploration as a reason for biting is on page 11 in chapter 1. Suggestions for strategies and techniques are on page 37 in chapter 3.

   ▶ Information on experimenting with cause and effect as a reason for biting is on page 11 in chapter 1. Suggestions for strategies and techniques are on pages 37–38 in chapter 3.

   ▶ Information on imitation as a reason for biting is on pages 11–12 in chapter 1. Suggestions for strategies and techniques are on page 38 in chapter 3.

Conclusion

Express your appreciation for people's participation. Let them know where they can bring any questions they may have. Let them know that all the details about these reasons are in *No Biting*, and tell them where they can find the book in your program.

Reasons Related to Development, Part 1

Possible reason	What you might see	What you can do when this is the reason
Teething pain/discomfort: Younger toddlers are often teething, and they gnaw on things for relief.		
Oral-motor development: Toddlers are exploring and experimenting with movement involving their mouths as they learn to talk, chew, and swallow. They often seek oral stimulation.		
Sensory exploration: Toddlers learn by exploring with their senses, including using their mouths to explore.		
Experimenting with cause and effect: Toddlers are learning about the results of their actions. "What happens when . . .?"		
Imitation: Toddlers use imitation as a way to learn. They may imitate adults who "play bite" them.		

MODULE 3 Why Toddlers Might Bite and Related Practices: Reasons Related to Development, Part 2

Overview of the Module

Module 3 continues looking at reasons toddlers might bite related to development. It includes how these reasons might be indicated and the strategies and techniques that work well when children bite for these reasons.

Objectives

▸ Participants will reflect on the importance of understanding why toddlers bite.

▸ Participants will study five reasons related to development that toddlers might bite and corresponding strategies and techniques to address them.

Segments

1. Review of module 2 and reflection on the importance of understanding why toddlers bite

2. Reasons related to developmental factors and practices to address them:
   - spatial awareness
   - emerging autonomy
   - expressive language development
   - need for attention
   - holding on and letting go

Preparation

Make copies of the module 3 handout for everyone. Tell participants that this is a working handout with a chart for their own ideas and notes. Read and become familiar with the sections on spatial awareness, emerging autonomy, expressive language development, need for attention, and holding on and letting go in chapter 3 of *No Biting*.

SEGMENT 1

Welcome everyone. Put the overview into your own words and share it with them. Begin by asking participants to complete this statement:

"What I thought was most important in module 2 about reasons toddlers bite was . . ."

Use their responses to have a short discussion and review of module 2.

SEGMENT 2

We'll be using the same process as in module 2 to look at additional reasons toddlers might bite that are related to development. Direct participants to the chart on the handout. Some boxes are filled in and others are not. Here again is how to use the chart to present, discuss, and work on these additional five reasons related to development. Participants will likely remember this process and the way the chart is set up.

1. Work on one reason at a time. Present the reason and the short explanation given in the box on the left. Check in with participants and ask how many of them are familiar with this.

   "In this first box, we see spatial awareness along with an explanation that toddlers are working on understanding how space works, and they do this by using their bodies."

   Here is a little more information about toddlers and spatial awareness. First, this is one of the most likely reasons toddlers might bite when they are in groups. Toddlers can't judge space by sight like we can as adults. A good example of how we do this as adults is our ability to pick the right size plastic container for leftovers—even when the cooking pot and the plastic container are different shapes and sizes. Let's contrast this with toddlers' ability to judge space. Here's a good example: they can't look at a space and figure out whether they would fit into it. To figure that out, they actually have to physically try to get into that space. This is why we so often see toddlers trying to go under things, go behind things, or squeeze into small spaces. We often have to help toddlers out of spaces they have gotten stuck in. Check in with participants and ask how many of them are familiar with this aspect of toddlers and spatial awareness.

   Additionally, since toddlers can't judge space by sight, when they go to sit down next to someone, they often end up sitting on top of the other child or half on top of the child. They also can't tell how close they really are to someone else or judge how close others are to them. They may be way too close to another child, and that child might protest loudly. Even when someone is not very close to them, toddlers might protest that they are. They simply don't have a good sense of how close or far away the other person is. As children get older, they do develop this sense of spatial awareness, but toddlers are in the "working on it" stage. Check in with participants and ask how many of them are familiar with this aspect of toddlers and spatial awareness.

Ask participants, "How might spatial awareness as we just described it result in a bite?" Give them time to respond. Again, this is crucial to the learning process because it helps participants make the connection between the reason and the actual bite.

2. Next, look at the middle box, "What you might see." Ask participants to think of what they might see that would indicate that the reason for a particular bite was related to spatial awareness. Ask them to write one of their ideas in the middle box, saving room for the ideas of other participants. Then ask participants to share their ideas with the group. Participants can create a list in that middle box as everyone shares their ideas. Here are some possible indicators. If all of these do not emerge from the group, add them yourself:

   • The child who bit was upset because another child was too close to him or her.

   • One child was literally on top of another, and the second child bit.

   • The child who bit was in a very crowded space.

   The indications above may be supported with more general observations of the child because they show the child to be someone who is really struggling with spatial awareness. Here are some examples of those more general observations:

   ▶ The child who bit often protests when others get too close to him or her.

   ▶ The child who bit often gets stuck in small spaces they try to get into.

   This is important because it helps participants understand that identifying the reason a toddler bites is a matter of observation.

3. Now look at the box on the right, "What you can do when this is the reason." This is the point at which we identify strategies and techniques that are directly related to the reason the child is biting, in this case spatial awareness.

Present the material directly from the section on spatial awareness in chapter 3 of *No Biting*. There are five specific suggestions in that section. They are worth a careful look for two reasons. First, as mentioned earlier, difficulty with spatial awareness is one of the most likely reasons toddlers bite. Second, the five suggestions given are very simple to implement; every toddler teacher should be aware of them. Encourage participants to write their own notes in the box on their handout. Ask them if they have additional ideas for that box, keeping in mind that the strategies and techniques must relate to spatial awareness.

Repeat this format for each of the other four reasons related to development on the handout. Here are the references in *No Biting* for each of the other reasons:

▸ Information on emerging autonomy as a reason for biting is on page 12 in chapter 1. Suggestions for strategies and techniques are on page 39 in chapter 3.

▸ Information on expressive language development as a reason for biting is on page 12 in chapter 1. Suggestions for strategies and techniques are on pages 39–40 in chapter 3. As you present this information and discuss it with participants, point out that the most effective way for toddlers to develop language is through one-on-one conversations with adults they know and trust. Here is a formula for these kinds of conversations. This is especially helpful because it is a wonderful technique to share with parents:

• Listen: Pay attention to what the child says, even if it's only a sound or one word.

• Repeat: Repeat what the child says.

• Add: Add a little more to what the child said. Don't ask a question.

• Wait: Wait for the child to respond and then go right back to "listen" and keep going.

▸ Information on the need for attention as a reason for biting is on pages 12–13 in chapter 1. Suggestions for strategies and techniques are on pages 40–41 in chapter 3. Note: This section of chapter 3 has a valuable discussion on the need for attention and specific suggestions on giving children individual attention in group settings. This is not only beneficial for a child who may be biting but also for all children.

▸ Information on holding on and letting go as a reason for biting is on page 13 in chapter 1. Suggestions for strategies and techniques are on page 41 in chapter 3.

Conclusion

Express your appreciation for people's participation. Let them know where they can bring any questions they may have. Let them know that all the details about the reasons and strategies and techniques are in *No Biting*, and tell them where they can find the book in your program.

Reasons Related to Development, Part 2

Possible reason	What you might see	What you can do when this is the reason
Spatial awareness: Toddlers are working on understanding how space works, and they do this by using their bodies.		
Emerging autonomy: Toddlers are experimenting with asserting themselves as independent beings who have some power and can control things and people.		
Expressive language development: Toddlers are working on developing verbal language, but they often are not able to express themselves with words.		
Need for attention: Toddlers seek interactions with adults for comfort and learning. If they do not get it, they may bite to get attention.		
Holding on and letting go: Toddlers' central nervous systems are developing so they can control their muscles that hold on and let go.		

MODULE 4 Why Toddlers Might Bite and Related Practices: Reasons Related to Expressing Feelings

Overview of the Module

Module 4 introduces participants to expression of feelings as another category of reasons toddlers might bite. In this module, we'll take an in-depth look at five specific reasons in this category.

Objectives

▶ Participants will examine expression of feelings as another category of reasons toddlers bite.

▶ Participants will study five reasons related to toddler biting and corresponding strategies and techniques.

Segments

1. Expression of feelings as a second category of reasons toddlers might bite

2. Reasons related to expressing feelings and practices to address them:

   • frustration and/or anger

   • tension

   • anxiety

   • excitement

   • self-protection

Preparation

Make copies of the module 4 handout for everyone. Remind participants that this is a working handout with a chart that includes information and room for their own ideas and notes. Read and become familiar with chapter 1, "Why Do Toddlers Bite?" and the sections on frustration, anger, tension, anxiety, and self-protection under "Strategies and Techniques Related to Expressing Feelings" in chapter 3 of *No Biting*.

SEGMENT 1

Welcome everyone. Put the overview into your own words and share it with them. Emphasize that the previous two modules were about reasons that toddlers might bite related to toddler development. In this module, we will be looking at reasons that fall into a different category, reasons that relate to expression of feelings.

SEGMENT 2

We'll be using the same process as in modules 2 and 3 to look at these reasons toddlers might bite that are related to expression of feelings. Direct participants to the chart on the handout. Again, some boxes are filled in and others are not. Here again is how to use the chart to present, discuss, and work on these additional five reasons related to development. Participants will likely remember this process and the way the chart is set up.

Work on one reason at a time. Present the reason and the short explanation given in the box on the left. Check in with participants and ask how many of them are familiar with this. "In this first box, we see frustration and anger along with an explanation that toddlers are struggling with a world that just doesn't always work the way they want it to. When they can't get what they want, they may lose control and lash out physically."

Here is a little more information about toddlers and frustration. Toddlers are driven to explore; one of their developmental tasks is to figure out how things work. Toddlers also learn through their own hands-on experiences. They want to do it themselves. Anyone who has worked with toddlers for more than one day has certainly been told in no uncertain terms, "Me do it!" Unfortunately, toddlers don't understand the difference between effort and ability. If there is something they want to do, they will attempt it even if they don't have the skills to do it. If they are not successful, they are often persistent. They continue to do exactly what isn't working, just with more and more force. We could hardly come up with a more perfect recipe for frustration. If we add in the toddler's limited ability to control their own emotions, it's pretty obvious how this is going to end. Here's an example. A toddler has a shape ball and is trying to put the round piece into the square hole. When it doesn't work, she pushes the round piece harder. When that doesn't work, she bangs the round piece onto the square hole. When that doesn't work, she bangs the round piece harder and harder and faster and faster onto the square hole. Finally, she slams the shape ball onto the floor and then kicks it as hard as she can.

Ask participants whether they have seen similar examples, and give them time to talk about their responses.

Here is a little more information about toddlers and frustration. Since toddlers are egocentric, they think that everyone sees things the same way they see them. They believe that everyone else wants the same things they want. "If I want a toy you have, you should want me to have that toy as well." When other people don't cooperate with what they want, they become frustrated. Just think for a moment of what this can look like in a group of toddlers where all of them have the same egocentric perspective. It's one of the realities behind our perspective statement, "When toddlers are in groups, biting is unfortunately not unexpected!"

Continue with a short activity that begins with this question for participants: "Consider your own experience with toddlers. Would you think that frustration is often a reason for toddler biting or rarely a reason for biting?" Let them respond and have a short discussion about their own experiences with how easily toddlers can become frustrated.

▶ Ask participants, "How might frustration as we just described it result in a bite?" Give them time to respond. Again, this is crucial to the learning process because it helps participants make the connection between the reason and the actual bite.

▶ Next, look at the middle box, "What you might see." Ask participants to think of what they might see that would indicate that the reason for a particular bite was related to frustration and anger. Give them one minute to list as many responses as possible. Have participants compare lists. Participants can create a list in that middle box as everyone shares their ideas. This is important because it helps participants understand that identifying the reason a toddler bites is a matter of observation.

▶ Now look at the box on the right, "What you can do when this is the reason." This is the point at which we identify strategies and techniques that are directly related to the reason the child is biting, in this case frustration or anger. Note that two categories are already given in that box: "What you can do to reduce possible frustration" and "How you can help a child who is getting frustrated." Present the material directly from the section on frustration and anger in chapter 3 of *No Biting*.

Here is an important consideration for this section. When we determine that the reason for biting is frustration, some of the suggested strategies and techniques given don't directly involve the child. However, they benefit the child and are important in helping reduce or prevent biting from frustration. These suggestions are a matter of protecting the child from undue frustration by making changes to the environment. This can include providing soothing water play, having duplicates of popular toys, and having toys and learning materials that pass the "Goldilocks standard"—that is, they are not so easy that they're boring, nor so difficult that toddlers don't stand much of a chance at being successful with them, but "just right." These suggestions provide a stark contrast to punishing toddlers for biting out of frustration. They are also far more likely to result in reducing biting from frustration. This has been mentioned again and again by toddler teachers who report that when they implemented the strategies and techniques related to frustration in their classrooms, biting decreased overall.

A related consideration here is that we do not punish the child who is so thoroughly frustrated or angry for biting. Rather, we help the child learn how to recover from these strong emotions. We also watch for signs that a child is becoming frustrated or angry, and we step in to help before the frustration or anger escalates and results in biting.

Encourage participants to write their own notes in the box on their handout. Ask them if they have additional ideas for that box, keeping in mind that the strategies and techniques must relate to frustration or anger.

Repeat this format for each of the other four reasons related to expression of feelings on the handout. Here are the references in *No Biting* for each of the other reasons:

▶ Information on tension as a reason for biting is on page 14 in chapter 1. Suggestions for strategies and techniques are on pages 42–43 in chapter 3.

▶ Information on anxiety as a reason for biting is on page 14 in chapter 1. Suggestions for strategies and techniques are on page 43 in chapter 3.

- A common response among many adults to the idea of toddler anxiety is "These kids are two years old! What do they have to feel anxious about?" There are two considerations here. First, there's a lot going on in a roomful of toddlers. Toddlers like things to be reliable and predictable, and this is not always the case in toddler classrooms. Children and caregivers change. The room might get rearranged. There might be a sudden change in the schedule. Toddlers are often in the potty-training process, which can be anxiety producing. Second, just as with adults, some toddlers are by nature more anxious than others. It's important to keep in mind that anxiety is individual. We must acknowledge toddler anxiety when we see toddlers exhibit it. Our role here is to help lessen those things that we know are associated with toddler anxiety.

- Note that there are two categories already given in the third box: "What you can do to reduce anxiety-producing situations" and "How you can help a child who is becoming anxious." These are written in specifically to help participants think in terms of both of those types of responses to biting when the reason is anxiety. Finally, note that as toddlers have more and more experiences where their initial anxiety does not result in something terrible happening, they develop confidence that they will be all right. This then helps relieve feelings of anxiety.

▸ Information on the need for excitement as a reason for biting is on page 14 in chapter 1. Suggestions for strategies and techniques are on page 43 in chapter 3. Note that there is a category already given in the third box: "Replacement behaviors that you might teach children." This helps remind us that we are not trying to change children's excitement but are helping them figure out what they can do when they are excited instead of biting.

▸ Information on self-protection as a reason for biting is on page 14 in chapter 1. There are no suggestions for strategies and techniques in chapter 3 because the best help we can offer a child who we believe is biting for this reason is a referral to an agency specifically designated to protect children and/or help families in these situations. This is not limited to a child who may be being abused. It includes children who may be experiencing or exposed to trauma. If and when teachers suspect this may be the case, they have probably already been speaking with their director and perhaps documenting the indicators of abuse or trauma.

Note that there are already two statements in the third box: "Referrals to outside agencies and how that works in our program" and "Consider suggestions related to frustration, anxiety, and tension that might help the child in the meantime."

Conclusion

Express your appreciation for people's participation. Let them know where they can bring any questions they may have. Let them know that all the details about these reasons and related strategies and techniques are in *No Biting*, and tell them where they can find the book in your program.

Reasons Related to Expressing Feelings

Possible reason	What you might see	What you can do when this is the reason
Frustration and anger: Toddlers are struggling with a world that just doesn't always work the way they want it to. When they can't get what they want, they may lose control and lash out physically.		What you can do to reduce possible frustration How you can help a child who is getting frustrated
Tension: When toddlers feel under pressure, their bodies can become very tense. Toddlers seek relief from this tension.		
Anxiety: Toddlers may feel insecure, scared, or confused and be unable to express or regulate those feelings. They may seek an oral solution.		What you can do to reduce anxiety-producing situations How you can help a child who is becoming anxious
Excitement: Toddlers are often not able to regulate their emotions and can easily become overexcited.		Replacement behaviors that you might teach children
Self-protection: Toddlers who are experiencing abuse or other trauma may be in an "alert to hurt" state.		Referrals to outside agencies and how that works in our program Consider suggestions related to frustration, anxiety, and tension that might help the child in the meantime.

MODULE 5 Why Toddlers Might Bite and Related Practices: Reasons Related to the Environment

Overview

Module 5 introduces participants to another category of reasons toddlers might bite—the way the environment works or doesn't work well for toddlers. In this module, we'll take an in-depth look at four specific reasons in this category and the strategies and techniques to address them.

Objectives

▶ Participants will examine aspects of the classroom environment as another category of reasons toddlers bite.

▶ Participants will study four reasons toddlers might bite that relate to the classroom environment and corresponding strategies and techniques to address them.

Segments

1. Aspects of the environment or program that are not working for the child as a category of reasons toddlers might bite

2. Reasons toddlers might bite related to the environment and practices to address them

   • an environment that is too stimulating or not stimulating enough

   • a space that is too crowded and does not allow children privacy

   • inappropriate expectations

   • a schedule that does not meet children's needs for food and sleep

Preparation

Make copies of the module 5 handout for everyone. Remind participants that this is a working handout with a chart that includes information and room for their own ideas and notes. Read and become familiar with chapter 1, "Why Do Toddlers Bite?" Note that sections in that chapter—"Provide a Supportive Environment," "Provide a Consistent Yet Flexible Schedule," and "Provide a Variety of Sensory Activities and Materials"—outline the strategies and practices related to the environment or program not working for the child.

SEGMENT 1

Welcome everyone. Put the overview into your own words and share it with them. Add the following: This category is quite different from the other two. The other two—reasons related to toddler development and reasons related to expressing feelings—are about the children themselves. This category is about the classroom environment. It relates to what the adults in the classroom do. It includes the space itself, the furnishings, and how the room is set up. It includes the toys and materials and the activities that are available for the children. It includes the expectations on them and the daily schedule. The suggestions for strategies and techniques in this category are where we can have the largest impact on helping prevent biting. Here is a real-life anecdote. An assistant director left her position at a child care center to become the director in a larger center nearby. She noticed that in the new center, the teachers used a great many more sensory activities and materials than in the center she had just left. She also noticed that the incidence of biting was much lower even though the center was larger.

SEGMENT 2

We'll be using the same process as in modules 2, 3, and 4 to look at these reasons toddlers might bite that are related to aspects of the environment. Direct participants to the chart on the handout. Again, some boxes are filled in and others are not. Here again is how to use the chart to present, discuss, and work on these additional five reasons related to development. Participants will likely remember this process and the way the chart is set up. There is one difference in this chart. The reasons themselves are self-explanatory, so there is no further explanation given in the first box for each reason.

1. Work on one reason at a time. Present the reason "an environment that is too stimulating or not stimulating enough" and ask participants to discuss what might make an environment too stimulating and then what might make an environment not stimulating enough.

....

Here is an example from a real-life toddler classroom. A toddler classroom that had been a bit chaotic was due to be repainted. Over the weekend, the husband of the program's owner decided to surprise her by painting the room. He knew his wife liked bright colors, so he painted the entire room—all four walls and the ceiling—neon blue. On Monday the room was no longer a bit chaotic; it was madly chaotic.

....

Ask participants, "How might an overstimulating environment as we just described it result in a bite?" "How might an environment that is not stimulating enough result in a bite?" Give them time to respond. Again, this is crucial to the learning process because it helps participants make the connection between the reason and the actual bite.

2. Next, look at the middle box, "What you might see." Ask participants to think of what they might see that would indicate that the reason for a particular bite was related to a child being either too stimulated by the environment or not stimulated enough. Participants can create a list in that middle box as everyone shares their ideas. This is important because it helps participants understand that identifying the reason a toddler bites is a matter of observation.

3. Now look at the box on the right, "What you can do when this is the reason." This is the point at which we identify strategies and techniques that are directly related to the reason the child is biting, in this case an environment that is too stimulating or not stimulating enough. Present the material directly from pages 16–18. Encourage participants to write their own notes in the box on their handout. Ask them if they have additional ideas for that box, keeping in mind that the strategies and techniques must relate to an environment that is too stimulating or not stimulating enough.

Here is a follow-up discussion activity. When it comes to the environment, we as the adults must make the changes. This is not always easy for some adults. Ask participants to consider and discuss this statement that was made by a toddler teacher. "I'm supposed to add more materials to the room because it's not stimulating enough for the children. But they just throw the toys around, so it doesn't make any sense. I'm not doing it!"

In the discussion, make sure the point is made that the adults must create an environment that meets the needs of the toddlers. Ask participants about their experiences helping toddlers interact with materials and how they organize cleaning up toys and materials.

Repeat this format for each of the other three reasons related to an environment or program that is not working for the child. Here are the references in *No Biting* for each of the other reasons:

▶ Information on "a space that is too crowded and does not allow for privacy" as a reason for biting is in chapter 1. Suggestions for strategies and practices are in the section "Provide a Supportive Environment," also in chapter 1.

Help participants recall the information about toddlers and spatial awareness from module 2. Here we can see how difficult it would be for children who are just developing spatial awareness to be in a room that is too crowded. And if there is no place for privacy, a child who is really overwhelmed has no place to go.

Think about this observation from many, many programs: even in classrooms where several children are biting at the same time, there is almost never any biting when they go outdoors. Ask participants what they think this indicates.

Here's another consideration. We often see children crowd together in certain areas of the room or around certain activities. Even though the room overall may not be crowded, certain spaces are. Ask participants to think of ways to make such areas less crowded.

▶ Information on inappropriate expectations as a reason for biting is in chapter 1. Suggestions for practices that are based on appropriate expectations of toddlers are listed and detailed in the section "Provide a Variety of Sensory Activities and Materials," also in chapter 1.

Ask participants to help create a list of the kinds of inappropriate expectations that toddlers might experience. If waiting and sharing are not mentioned, bring them up yourself in the discussion.

Most participants will have experience with toddlers and waiting. And it will come as no surprise that it is inappropriate to expect toddlers to wait patiently. This is covered well in *No Biting* under "Provide a Consistent Yet Flexible Schedule" in chapter 1.

Sharing is a tough one because we all want young children to learn to share. Most of the time we don't think about learning to share as a process; we simply expect it to happen. Since sharing is a positive behavior, it's difficult to think of it as an inappropriate expectation. It helps to remind ourselves that *inappropriate* here means "not a good match for toddlers." The expectation that toddlers must share doesn't match toddler development or the way toddlers think. This is mostly because one of the main developmental tasks of toddlers is to understand themselves as autonomous and to practice becoming so. This is why we so often hear toddlers stand up for themselves while loudly proclaiming, "Mines!" Sharing doesn't really fit into this picture.

If we want children to learn to share, we have to understand the process of learning to share. First, children need to understand ownership. "This is *your* nose, and this is *my* nose." "This is *Sara's* hat, and that one is *your* hat." Then children can learn that ownership can go back and forth. They learn this when they roll a ball to another person who rolls it back. This is a great activity for teachers to do with children because the teacher can be trusted to roll the ball back. Then toddlers can learn that they can play with something for a longer time, then someone else can play with it, and they'll then get it back. It's when they have established a belief that they will "get it back" that they can really share. And this usually happens when they are preschoolers.

▶ Information on "a schedule that does not meet children's needs for food, sleep, and activity" is in chapter 1. Suggestions for practices related to this possible reason for biting are in the section "Provide a Consistent Yet Flexible Schedule," also in chapter 1. There are special challenges for meeting the needs of individual children in group settings.

Ask participants to think of ways in which they have made modifications to the schedule and how they realized changes were needed. Also ask them when they might have adjusted the schedule to meet the needs of a particular child. Use these as points of discussion.

Conclusion

Express your appreciation for people's participation. Let them know where they can bring any questions they may have. Let them know that all the details about these reasons and the corresponding strategies and techniques are in *No Biting*, and tell them where they can find the book in your program.

Reasons Related to the Environment

Possible reason	What you might see	What you can do when this is the reason
An environment that is too stimulating or not stimulating enough		
A space that is too crowded and does not allow for privacy		
Inappropriate expectations		
A schedule that does not meet children's needs for food, sleep, and activity		

MODULE 6 Responding When Toddlers Bite

Overview of the Module

Module 6 focuses on what to do in the moments after a child bites. This is what most toddler caregivers want to know. All the information from the previous modules form the foundation for responding to biting right when it happens.

Objectives

▸ Participants will know specific steps to help them clue in to biting situations so they can respond effectively.

▸ Participants will know how to respond to the child who was bitten.

▸ Participants will know how to respond to the child who bit.

Segments

1. Responding when toddlers bite—cluing in to the situation

2. Helping the child who was bitten

3. Helping the child who bit

Preparation

Make copies of the module 6 handout for everyone. Let participants know that this is a working handout with an outline and room for them to take their own notes. Read and become familiar with chapter 2, "What to Do When Toddlers Bite," in *No Biting*. The outline on the handout follows the curriculum point by point.

SEGMENT 1

Welcome everyone. Put the overview into your own words and share it with them. Here is a statement directly from *No Biting*: "Whenever you're dealing with biting, you need to act quickly and directly. You want your words, attitudes, and actions to convey a strong message:

▸ Biting is not the right thing to do.

▸ You will help the child who was bitten feel better.

▸ You will help the child who bit learn and practice different, more appropriate behavior."

This begins with a quick assessment of the situation based on what you can observe.

1. Clue in to the situation.

2. What has happened? You may not actually see the bite, but from what you *can* observe, you can often get a good idea of what happened. Ask participants what they think might have happened if they realize a bite has just taken place . . .

   - and they look up and see one child crying and rubbing her arm, and another child standing nearby holding a favorite doll up in the air.
   - and they look up and see one child in a toddler wagon and the other child half in and half out of the wagon with a bite on his face.

   Ask what other scenarios they may have encountered in their own experience. What did they see and what did they decide probably happened?

3. Where are the children? Are the child who bit and the child who was bitten still in close proximity? Has the child who bit already wandered off? Are the children in physical contact with each other?

   - Short discussion: Ask participants to think about and discuss how this information might help them clue in to the situation.

4. What is the stress level of the situation? Are either or both of the children crying, screaming, or showing other indications of heightened emotion? Are either or both of the children vocalizing—whether through actual words or "toddlerese"—in an emphatic, indignant, loud voice? Is one child pursuing the other? Are the children physically grappling with each other?

   - Short discussion: Again, ask participants to think about and discuss how this information might help them clue in to the situation and decide how to respond.

5. Determine who to go to first. Unless the child who bit is in danger of hurting someone else, go to the child who was bitten first. Attend to that child first, and then go to the child who bit. Ideally, the child who bit should see you attend to the child who was bitten. If the child who bit seems out of control, attend to that child first, helping him or her become calm. If two staff members are available, decide who will go to which child. Sometimes a child has a closer relationship with a particular caregiver. If that is the case in the biting situation, the staff person with the closest relationship with a child should go to that child. This is especially helpful in approaching the child who bit.

SEGMENT 2

Show participants how to help the child who was bitten feel better by providing

- ▶ Physical care. Refer to the information on first aid for bites on pages 21–22.

- ▶ Comfort care and empathy. Refer to the first paragraph under "Helping the Child Who Was Bitten" in chapter 2. Pay special attention to the statements that express empathy and discuss why that's important. Ask participants about the kinds of things they do to comfort children who are upset in general and which of these might work especially well when a child has been bitten.

  - • Short activity: Direct participants to the italicized dialogue on the handout about expressing empathy. Discuss with them how these statements indicate that the adult empathizes with the child. Also note that in one example, the adult says, "I'm sorry . . ." This is important because it sends the message that the adult feels bad about the situation, and this matters to the child. A heartfelt "I'm sorry this happened" from a caring adult is far more effective than a forced "I'm sorry" from the child who bit—if that child can even talk yet!

- ▶ Advice and support. Refer to the remainder of the section "Helping the Child Who Was Bitten." Much of this information refers to helping the child learn how he can respond and stand up for himself if and when someone bites him. Note that this does not mean we expect toddlers to be responsible for their own safety, but rather to help a child who was bitten understand that he can take action himself. This is important for toddlers who are in the process of developing a sense of autonomy, one of the primary tasks of toddlerhood.

SEGMENT 3

Help the child who bit by using the following strategies:

- ▶ Biting is never the right thing to do. Refer to "Helping the Child Who Bit" section in chapter 2.

- ▶ Express just strong enough disapproval. It is important that toddlers be able to tell by the tone of your voice that biting is not the right thing to do. So you want it to sound serious, but you don't want it to sound threatening or harsh.

- Short activity: Direct participants to the sub-bulleted list on the handout, which is about sending such a message. Ask them how and why this approach is more likely to be effective than responding in a loud, harsh manner. Also ask them whether this kind of response comes easily to adults. Does it come easily to them? If not, and if we realize that it's more effective, then how can we learn to use this approach?

▶ Be brief, genuine, and serious. This refers to the actual words we use when first speaking to the child. The "brief" part is important because toddlers are very unlikely to pay attention to a long, detailed explanation of what they just did and why it's wrong. We wish they would, but they won't. All toddler caregivers are familiar with this reality. Our words and tone need to reflect our genuine conviction that biting is not the right thing to do, and that this is serious. This builds on the previous point about expressing disapproval.

  - Short activity: Ask participants to listen to two examples of such statements. Do these one at a time. Ask participants to note that each statement is very brief. You may actually ask someone to time each one. They will realize that each of these statements takes only seconds to say. Then ask them how the words send a genuine and serious message. (Of course, you must use a genuine and serious voice.)

  - "You bit him with your teeth. He doesn't like it. It's not all right to bite people." (You can note that adding the words "with your teeth" clarifies the word "bit" for very young toddlers.)

  - "You bit her, and it hurt her. That's why she's crying. I don't want you to bite anyone."

▶ Use a response and language that fits the specific situation. Adding a brief, specific description of what happened is helpful for toddlers because they can almost always understand more than they can express. It also helps us avoid general statements, such as "Biting is not nice." While true, this is too vague to be effective. It is helpful to be specific by using the name of the child who was bitten rather than referring to "your friends."

  - Short activity: Direct participants to the italicized dialogue on the handout, which is an example of an actual response. Discuss with participants what it is about this response that makes it fit a specific situation. How is it different from saying, "You shouldn't bite. That's not nice"?

Help the child who bit learn and practice different, more appropriate behavior:

▶ Use a response that fits the situation.

- Advice and modeling: Refer to the section "Tie Your Verbal Response to an Action Response" in chapter 2. When presenting this information, consider starting with the example of Anna and Malik from the text. Ask participants to comment on the approach of the caregiver. Then go on to present the information on helping a child learn the words, tone of voice, and body language to express strong feelings such as anger. Be sure to talk about ways to support the child as he or she tries out and practices this new skill.

- Redirection: Refer to the section "Redirection" in chapter 2 on page 26.

- Short activity: Direct participants to the italicized dialogue on the handout, which is an example of redirection. Ask participants why they think this response starts with a "You wish . . ." statement. Note that it sets up the reality statement that comes next. Ask participants to look at the two choices for what the child can do next. What do they notice about those choices? Why doesn't the response just ask them what they want to do?

- Don't let children profit from biting. This concept is usually easy to understand. Direct participants to the italicized dialogue on the handout. Ask them to discuss how the statement clearly conveys the idea that this child is not going to profit from biting.

▸ Structure specific, supervised situations to be "bite-free." This is a very specific strategy that is especially helpful when one child has bitten another child several times. Rather than trying to keep the two children apart, structure a soothing sensory activity such as water play. Bring both children to the water table, and position yourself between them while they play. The value of this activity is that it allows both children to experience time together when biting does not happen.

Conclusion

Express your appreciation for people's participation. Let them know where they can bring any questions they may have. Let them know that all the details about this topic are in *No Biting*, and tell them where they can find the book in your program.

Responding when Young Children Bite

Clue In to the Situation

- ▶ What has happened?

- ▶ Where are the children?

- ▶ What is the stress level of the situation?

- ▶ Determine who to go to first.

Help the Child Who Was Bitten Feel Better

- ▶ Give physical care.

- ▶ Provide comfort care and empathy: *"Oh no, you were bitten. That hurts so much." "I'm sorry he bit you. It's not right, and it's not fair."*

- ▶ Offer advice and support.

Help the Child Who Bit

- ▶ State that biting is never the right thing to do.

- ▶ Express just strong enough disapproval.

  - • This works best when you have already established a warm, positive relationship with the child.

  - • Talk with the child privately and at his eye level.

  - • Speak a little softer and more slowly than usual; use a serious voice and face.

- ▶ Be brief, genuine, and serious.

- ▶ Use a response and language that fits the specific situation: *"You were so mad when the truck wouldn't work! And you bit Trey. Biting hurts. I'll help you when you're mad, but you may not bite people."*

Learning and Practicing Different, More Appropriate Behavior

- ▶ Use a response that fits the situation:

  - • advice and modeling

  - • redirection: *"You wish you could stay here and get into the cubby with Tyrone. But only one person can be in the cubby at a time. You can go to a different cubby, or you can play with the trucks."*

  - • don't let children profit from biting: *"Emmy had a toy you wanted, and you bit her to take it away. Biting hurts people, and you can't have toys when you bite people to get them."*

- ▶ Structure specific, supervised situations to be "bite-free."

MODULE 7 Our Program's Policies and Procedures

Overview of the Module

Module 7 discusses why policies and procedures related to biting are important and gives participants the opportunity to review their own program's biting policy and procedures.

Objectives

- ▸ Participants will understand the role of policies and procedures when it comes to biting.

- ▸ Participants will read and review their program's policy on biting.

- ▸ Participants will review their program's procedures related to biting.

Segments

1. The role of policies and procedures

2. This program's policy on biting

3. This program's procedures related to biting

Preparation

Read and be familiar with the first four paragraphs of "Developing Policies about Biting" in chapter 6 of *No Biting* for segment 1. You will also need your center's biting policy in writing and your center's procedures related to biting. For this module, you have some choices for the handout:

- ▸ You can make copies of your center's written policy and written procedures related to biting and use those instead of the handout.

- ▸ You can insert your center's policy and your center's procedures related to biting into the module 7 handout.

SEGMENT 1

Welcome everyone.

Policies are decisions made ahead of time. Having a policy means that we have already decided how to handle something that we can reasonably expect to happen. Since we already acknowledge that "when toddlers are in groups, biting is unfortunately not unexpected," we can reasonably anticipate that there may be biting in our program. When it does happen, our policy is already in place to guide how we respond. The danger of not having a policy is that when biting occurs, we don't have a decision already made, and we are likely to act out of a default mode. That usually means that we end up doing whatever occurs to us at the moment. Such actions are likely to be very inconsistent. And if someone pressures us, we may give in to that pressure whether it's a good course of action or not. This is not very professional, and it usually doesn't feel good. A written policy that is clear and well thought out will help ensure that biting will be dealt with appropriately and consistently.

When is a policy not a policy? When it simply states that biting will be dealt with on a case-by-case basis. In this instance, a program doesn't have any preparation for responding to biting. And this makes no sense since we can reasonably expect that biting may well happen. Use the firefighter analogy from chapter 6 to stress this concept.

If you are using the module 7 handout, direct participants to the talking point at the top. Talking points are statements that are compact, clearly expressed, and persuasive; they are concise messages with an important purpose. Talking points are not written in formal academic language. Rather, they are written in the same way we would talk informally. In *No Biting*, this is the talking point about the value of a biting policy. Ask participants to look at that talking point and see if someone will volunteer to read it aloud. It's fine if no one does; you can read it aloud. Then ask participants, "What is this talking point's important purpose? How does it get its point across?"

▶ If you are not using the module 7 handout, present the information about talking points, and then read the talking point to participants:

• The words *policies* and *biting* just don't seem like they belong together. And yet we have a biting policy, and we're glad we do. We took the time to learn about biting, to think about all the issues, and to decide what to do when it happens. This has turned out to be very helpful. Our policy steers us away from bad decisions, keeps everyone on the same page, and sets us on the best path for children.

Procedures are the ways we carry out the program; they are what we actually do. Ask participants to respond to this question: "Why is it so important to have procedures in dealing with biting?" As participants respond, listen for these especially important reasons. If no one mentions them, raise them yourself:

▶ to make sure everyone knows what to do

▶ to make sure no steps are forgotten

▶ to make sure there is consistency throughout the program

SEGMENT 2

Present your program's policy on biting and review it with participants. It is often helpful to explain how the policy was developed. Where is your policy written? How are parents informed about the policy? Note any components of the policy that apply specifically to staff. Especially highlight the program's policy on confidentiality—that is, not revealing the identity of the child who is biting.

SEGMENT 3

Present and review your program's procedures related to biting. As you do this, check in with participants to ensure that the procedures are clear. Listen for indications that participants are surprised or not familiar with specific procedures, and spend more time on those.

Talk about how procedures are updated and then communicated with staff:

▶ Short activity: Ask participants to consider and discuss this question: "In what ways might it be difficult to follow these procedures?" The purpose of this activity is to discover whether there are barriers to following the procedures, and, if there are, how to overcome those barriers.

▶ Short activity: Ask participants to share any tips they have for carrying out specific procedures. Some of the best suggestions come from the people who do the work every day.

Conclusion

Express your appreciation for people's participation. Let them know where they can bring any questions they may have. Let them know that they can read more about this topic in *No Biting,* and tell them where they can find the book in your program.

A Talking Point on Biting Policies

The words *policies* and *biting* just don't seem like they belong together. And yet we have a biting policy, and we're glad we do. We took the time to learn about biting, to think about all the issues, and to decide what to do when it happens. This has turned out to be very helpful. Our policy steers us away from bad decisions, keeps everyone on the same page, and sets us on the best path for children.

Our Program's Policy Related to Biting:

Our Program's Procedures Related to Biting:

MODULE 8 Working with Parents When Toddlers Bite

Overview of the Module

Module 8 helps participants learn how to work effectively with parents when toddlers are biting. It begins with understanding parents' perspectives on biting and then includes suggestions for working with parents of the child who bit, parents of the child who was bitten, and parents of other children in the program.

Objectives

▸ Participants will understand how parents look at biting and why this matters.

▸ Participants will learn to work effectively with parents of children who were bitten.

▸ Participants will learn to work effectively with parents of children who bite.

▸ Participants will learn to work with the parents of other children in the program.

Segments

1. Understanding parents' perspectives on biting

2. Working with parents of children who are bitten

3. Working with parents of children who bite

4. Working with parents of other children in the program

Preparation

Make copies of the module 8 handout for everyone. Let participants know that this handout has information so they won't have to try to write down everything themselves as well as room for them to take their own notes. Read and become familiar with chapter 4, "Working with Parents and Other Community Members" in *No Biting*.

SEGMENT 1

Welcome everyone. Put the overview into your own words and share it with them. Direct participants to the chart at the top of the handout. Review and discuss it together. Give participants the opportunity to add any other differences they have noticed or experienced. Then ask participants to respond to this question: "Why does it matter that caregivers and parents look at biting differently?"

Conclude this segment with the understanding that it's important for caregivers and directors to acknowledge parents' perspectives. *Acknowledge* doesn't mean *agree with* but rather that we accept that this is how parents look at biting. When we understand parents' thinking about biting, we are better able to understand the depth of their feelings. We can also understand their reactions and suggestions. This helps us understand how best to work effectively with parents when toddlers are biting.

SEGMENT 2

Use the bullets from the handout as the structure for this segment. Use the material from "Helping the Parents of the Child Who Is Being Bitten" from chapter 4 in *No Biting* as you present this segment.

Acknowledge and respect the parents' feelings and the depth of those feelings. Parents may be angry and demanding when biting first occurs. Talk with participants about understanding and responding to this anger. Note that for all people, our brains process emotion before processing thoughts and reason. So we can't ignore the strong feelings parents may express when biting first happens. We need to acknowledge them before we can expect parents to hear and absorb information. Also discuss the inevitable parent demand for the name of the child who bit. All of this is covered in chapter 4, including carefully thought-out responses.

Tell them how you will help keep their child safe. This might involve increased supervision. It might also involve helping the child learn to stand up for himself or herself as discussed in module 6 and covered in chapter 2. Note that it might also include changes you have made to the environment or to activities that will help decrease biting. Giving parents specific details of what you are actually doing is much more helpful than general statements that are true but vague.

Tell them what you are doing to teach the child who bit not to bite anymore. This is where all the work in previous modules pays off. Caregivers will have some good ideas of what strategies and techniques to use with the child who bit, and they can share that with the parents of the child who was bitten. Many parents appreciate that their caregivers have a good idea of what to do that may help the biting stop. Again, giving specific details is more helpful than general statements. Caregivers need to be mindful, however, not to reveal the identity of the child who is biting.

Conclude this segment with the understanding that participants may need to refer parents to the program's director. This could happen if parents have very specific demands or suggestions that call for decisions or responses only the director can make.

SEGMENT 3

Use the bullets from the handout as the structure for this segment. Use the material from "Helping the Parents of the Child Who Is Biting" from chapter 4 in *No Biting* as you present this segment.

Parents who have experienced having both a child who was bitten and one who did the biting often say they felt more helpless in the second situation! Some parents want to know what they can do at home. In truth, however, most of the work with the child who bites will be done in the program because that's where he or she is biting. At the same time, it is important to support parents who want to be involved in helping their child. Here are some suggestions for them. As you talk with parents about these suggestions, tell them how these relate to biting. It gives the suggestions added meaning:

> **Help the child develop language**. These suggestions would be the same as those for caregivers in chapter 3 and covered in module 3 under language development as a reason related to biting. Review these with participants. Emphasize with parents that the most effective way to help toddlers develop language is through back-and-forth conversations. This is both doable for parents and effective for the child.

> **Stop "play biting" ("I could just eat you up!"), at least for a time**. This is covered in chapter 3 and discussed in module 2 under "imitation as a reason for biting." Many parents appreciate this particular suggestion because it makes so much sense, and it is relatively easy to do.

> **Model appropriate ways to express feelings**. Parents can understand and appreciate that their child tries to imitate them. They may even have some humorous or touching anecdotes of this behavior. To capitalize on this, help parents think about how they can model expressing feelings, especially strong feelings such as anger. Then consider with them what their toddler sees when they, as parents, express anger. This might be a good time for "conspicuous modeling"—that is, creating and using very purposeful responses specifically so children can see them and have a good model to imitate. These responses should combine words, tone of voice, and body language to express anger in a way that comes across as genuine and definite but isn't verbally or physically threatening. Here's an example of such conspicuous modeling. When a parent is upset or frustrated, she can use an emphatic tone of voice to say, "Oh no! That drawer just broke. That's so frustrating!" The parent can add emphatic body language by putting her hands on her hips or crossing her arms over her chest with great gusto. In this instance, the parent says she's frustrated,

she sounds frustrated, and she looks frustrated, but she doesn't hurt anyone. It is valuable for the parent to then take a deep breath to model how she can recover from this strong feeling after expressing it. If the child starts imitating the parent to express strong feelings, the parent can reinforce this by saying, "I could tell that you were really mad. Good for you."

▶ **Model caring, empathetic behavior.** This again builds on the way toddlers use imitation to learn. Let parents know that the more their child can understand the feelings of others, the easier it will be to help him or her stop biting. It's important to note that this happens best when toddlers see adults who are important to them model caring, empathetic behavior. Toddlers need to hear their parents use simple words of caring and empathy, such as "Are you okay?" coupled with gentle, caring actions like a pat on the arm or offering a tissue. And, again, parents should show their approval and pleasure when their toddler shows the same kind of empathy and caring behavior.

▶ **Express disapproval for biting if the child bites at home.** Help participants review this information from the module 6 handout on sending such a message. Here is how to send a disapproving message about biting:

- This works best when you have already established a warm, positive relationship with the child.

- Talk with the child privately and at his eye level.

- Speak a little softer and more slowly than usual; use a serious voice and face.

SEGMENT 4

Use the bullets from the handout as the structure for this segment. Use the material from "Working with Parents of Other Children in the Program" from chapter 4 in *No Biting* as you present this segment.

Here is how to help parents of other children in the program:

▶ **Keep them informed about what is happening related to the biting.** Parents almost always know that something related to biting is going on. Caregivers need to work with their program director to decide how to talk with parents about what is happening. Parents appreciate some acknowledgment from the program about the biting; it shows that the program is not trying to hide the situation. At the same time, caregivers and the director must make sure to keep the identity of the child(ren) who bit and other specific details confidential.

▸ **Tell them what you are doing to protect children from biting.** This usually involves changes in supervision and perhaps changes to the environment and activities that will help prevent or reduce some of the biting. Caregivers need to work with their program director to create this message and share it with parents. Sharing the specific steps you are taking is much more helpful than general statements such as "We are working very hard on this situation."

▸ **Give them specific suggestions they can use at home with their own children.** This mostly involves listening to their children and taking their cue from them. If their child does not talk about the biting, they shouldn't pump the child for information. If their child expresses concern about the biting, parents can tell her, "We'll tell Teacher Lucy that you're worried, and she will help you." This may seem as though the parent is passing the buck here. But, in reality, the biting is taking place in the classroom, and the person who is in the classroom is Teacher Lucy. The parent is also expressing confidence in Teacher Lucy, a confidence that the child can sense and take comfort in.

Conclusion

Express your appreciation for people's participation. Let them know where they can bring any questions they may have. Let them know that they can read more about this topic in *No Biting,* and tell them where they can find the book in your program.

When it comes to biting, caregivers . . .	When it comes to biting, parents . . .
are not surprised when toddlers bite;	are usually very surprised—sometimes even shocked—when toddlers bite;
know that biting is not unusual behavior for toddlers and doesn't necessarily indicate that something is seriously wrong;	assume something must be terribly wrong, either with the child or with the program, when toddlers bite;
know toddlers bite for many reasons;	may see toddler biting as a deliberate act of aggression;
know it may take some time for the biting to stop;	believe that biting can be stopped quickly and easily;
know they can't guarantee there will be no biting.	believe biting can be "guaranteed against."

Helping Parents of Children Who Are Being Bitten

Here are some ways to help the parents of children who are being bitten:

▶ Acknowledge and respect the parents' feelings and the depth of those feelings.

▶ Tell them how you will help keep their child safe.

▶ Tell them what you are doing to teach the child who bit not to bite anymore.

Helping Parents of Children Who Are Biting

Parents who have experienced having both a child who was bitten and one who did the biting often say they felt more helpless in the second situation! While most of the work with a child who bites will be done in the program, parents may ask what they can do at home. Here are some suggestions for them:

▶ Help the child develop language.

▶ Stop "play biting" ("I could just eat you up!"), at least for a time.

▶ Model appropriate ways to express feelings.

▶ Model caring, empathetic behavior.

▶ Express disapproval for biting if the child bites at home.

Helping Parents of Other Children in the Program

Here are some ways to help the parents of other children in the program:

▶ Keep them informed about what is happening related to the biting.

▶ Tell them what you are doing to protect children from biting.

▶ Give them specific suggestions they can use at home with their own children.

Role-Playing to Help Staff Build Skills

Directors have asked for suggestions to use role playing to help build teachers' communication skills with parents during biting incidents and episodes. Role-playing can be beneficial because it gives participants the opportunity to take the perspective of another person and to practice formulating appropriate responses. Role-playing can also be difficult because many people hesitate or even decline to participate; they don't like being put on the spot. And sometimes it's difficult because a participant may take the role play off course by creating an exaggerated character who is unreasonable and unpredictable.

Here is a version of role playing that works a little differently. It is designed as a staff development activity for a small group of four to six people. It produces even more benefits than traditional role playing. Participants work together, thinking in depth about the role they're playing and carefully crafting effective responses. No one is put on the spot; everyone participates. No one person can take the role play off course; everyone helps think through responses. Finally, there is a time for reflection, which is always helpful in building skills.

The director has a vital role in this staff development activity. First, the director introduces the activity and therefore needs to understand it thoroughly. Second, the director facilitates the role play. As the facilitator, you decide when to help the participants, when to ask them to explain their decisions, and when to have them reflect on their decisions. Finally, the director leads a short reflection at the end of the activity. The paragraph below describes this version of role playing and is written as a ready-to-use introductory script. Note that it refers to two people working together. If there are six people, there would be three people working together.

Groups don't have to be the same size, so two people could work together as the parent, and the other three people could work together as the teacher.

. . . .

"This is a slightly different way to do role playing. There are still two roles, the parent and the teacher. But in this version, you are not alone. There will be two or three of you who will work as a team to play each of the roles. One team will work together to be the parent, to think like the parent and decide what he or she might say. The other team will work together to be the teacher and to decide on appropriate responses to the parent. The team working as the parent needs to think about the parent's perspective and speak from that point of view. The team that's working as the teacher is already familiar with the teacher's perspective. Their job is to listen to the parent and then create a response that is respectful and is also based on good information about biting."

. . . .

Here's how the activity unfolds:

1. Once everyone understands the process, the facilitator begins the activity with a "parent prompt," a statement from a parent that starts the role play. Here are examples of some parent prompts to start the role play. These are all real-life examples, and you may well have some of your own. If you do, make sure they are situations a teacher would discuss with parents and not an issue for the director.

   - "I know there's a biter in the room. Could you just keep my daughter away from the biter so she won't get bitten?"

   - "What are you doing to punish the child who bit my son? We both know that kids have to learn that biting is not acceptable. And I tell you, nothing works better than a good punishment."

   - "I told my son that if someone bites him, he should bite them back. That's what I did when my brother bit me, and my mother said he never bit again."

   - "I read your incident report, and I saw that my daughter bit the child who took a toy away from her. I really feel this should be considered a justified bite and that there's no need to do anything about it. Don't you agree?"

   - "I'm so worried about my son. This is the third time he's been bitten. Isn't there anything you can do to keep him safe?"

2. Then the team playing the role of the teacher will talk among themselves and decide on a response.

3. The conversation then goes back to the parent. The team playing that role will talk among themselves to decide how they would like to respond to the teacher's comment.

4. This exchange continues, going back and forth. It creates a conversation between the parent and the teacher. During the role play, you can write out the conversation as it develops on chart paper or on a laptop. This helps keep track of the conversation and allows you to save conversations for reflection later.

5. As the conversation evolves, the facilitator can help participants think more about their roles and their comments and responses. You might ask the team playing the parent role about a particular comment or response from the teachers and how it felt to them. You might ask the team playing the teacher how they came up with a particular response. Use this when you would like participants to think a little more deeply about their role and their responses.

6. There is no predetermined length for this role play. The value is in the process, not in any particular end result. You can end it at any point, but save some time for a few reflection questions. You can also pick up the role play at a later time if you and the staff want to continue working on it.

7. Conclude the activity with questions for self-reflection. Here are some examples:

   • What was it like for you to participate in this role play?

   • What, if anything, was difficult for you in the role you played—either the parent or teacher? Why was it difficult?

   • What did you learn that might be helpful to you in real-life situations?

   • What would you like to say about being the parent? About being the teacher?

This version of role playing does not go quickly, but it produces less anxiety and a higher-quality conversation than the traditional version. It generates a great deal of discussion, thinking, and learning. This is a meaningful staff development activity because it can be done in short time frames and requires almost no preparation. In addition, this version of role playing can be used again and again with different prompts. Directors may have trusted, experienced staff members who can serve as facilitators.